Series/Number 07-112

TREE MODELS OF SIMILARITY AND ASSOCIATION

JAMES E. CORTER
Teachers College, Columbia University

SAGE PUBLICATIONS
International Educational and Professional Publisher
Thousand Oaks   London   New Delhi

For information address:

 SAGE Publications, Inc.
2455 Teller Road
Thousand Oaks, California 91320
E-mail: order@sagepub.com

SAGE Publications Ltd.
6 Bonhill Street
London EC2A 4PU
United Kingdom

SAGE Publications India Pvt. Ltd.
M-32 Market
Greater Kailash I
New Delhi 110 048 India

Printed in the United States of America

Library of Congress Catalog Card No. 89-043409

Corter, James E.
  Tree models of similarity and association / author, James E.
Corter.
    p.   cm.—Quantitative applications in the social sciences; vol. 07-112)
  Includes bibliographical references.
  ISBN 0-8039-5707-6 (pbk.: acid-free paper)
  1. Scaling (Social sciences)   I. Title.   II. Series: Sage
university papers series. Quantitative applications in the social
sciences; no. 07-112.
  H61.27.C67   1996
  300'.1'5195—dc20   95-50165

This books is printed on acid-free paper.

96 97 98 99 00 01   10 9 8 7 6 5 4 3 2 1

Sage Production Editor: Gillian Dickens
Sage Typesetter: Andrea D. Swanson

When citing a university paper, please use the proper form. Remember to cite the current Sage University Paper series title and include the paper number. One of the following formats can be adapted (depending on the style manual used):

(1) CORTER, JAMES E. (1996) Tree Models of Similarity and Association. Sage University Paper series on Quantitative Applications in the Social Sciences, 07-112. Thousand Oaks, CA: Sage.

OR

(2) Corter, J. E. (1996) *Tree models of similarity and association* (Sage University Paper series on Quantitative Applications in the Social Sciences, series no. 07-112). Thousand Oaks, CA: Sage.

CONTENTS

SERIES EDITOR'S INTRODUCTION

In this series, we have a number of papers that treat multivariate techniques for scaling or dimensional analysis. Certain titles have obvious relevance: *Multidimensional Scaling* (No. 11) by Kruskal and Wish; *Cluster Analysis* (No. 44) by Aldenderfer and Blashfield; *Three-Way Scaling and Clustering* (No. 65) by Arabie, Carroll, and DeSarbo; *Principal Components Analysis* (No. 69) by Dunteman; *Metric Scaling* (No. 75) by Weller and Romney; *Data Theory and Dimensional Analysis* (No. 78) by Jacoby; and *Typologies and Taxonomies* (No. 102) by Bailey. This monograph by Dr. Corter is another useful addition to this methodological line. Tree models may be thought of as graphics for, or from, a cluster analysis. For example, we might have an ultrametric tree model fitted through a hierarchical clustering routine.

Tree modeling applies to a broad category of data—proximity data. For example, suppose a political scientist wishes to evaluate the similarity of pairs of candidates running for office, as judged by a sample of voters. He or she may analyze the data with more traditional techniques, such as principal components or multidimensional scaling. Tree modeling, an alternative to these more standard scaling techniques, also might be applied. In Chapter 2, Dr. Corter explicates two types of trees: ultrametric and additive. The tree structure reveals the similar pairings, and the arc lengths themselves can add to the interpretation. Additive trees may be either rooted or unrooted, and that decision is as important as whether to rotate the matrix in a factor analysis.

Several algorithms for fitting trees to data exist, including the widely available agglomerative clustering routines, useful for building an ultrametric tree. Satisfactory algorithms for additive trees are more difficult to come by, but one is described helpfully in Appendix B. There are several pragmatic issues to be faced, one of which is how to assess goodness of fit. In Appendix C, Dr. Corter develops a useful, R^2 measure for evaluating the fit of a given tree solution.

By way of exposition, two well-chosen examples are detailed, one on organizational structure, another on perceived societal risk. In the first, members of university departments within a college are asked to select which departments they should be combined with in a college reorganization. The tree modeling of these proximity data, based on a hierarchical clustering procedure (average linkage between groups, in SPSS), yielded a dendrogram with three large groupings. It is interesting that these groupings do not correspond to the current divisions of the college. The implication is that the formal organization does not conform with the actual organization. One question is whether a spatial technique, such as multidimensional scaling, would lead to the same conclusion. The answer is, not necessarily. Tree models can give different results from spatial techniques. Thus, they are capable of providing unique insights into data structure.

—*Michael S. Lewis-Beck*
Series Editor

TREE MODELS OF SIMILARITY AND ASSOCIATION

JAMES E. CORTER
Teachers College, Columbia University

1. INTRODUCTION

Purpose of the Book and Its Relation to the Scaling Literature

Clustering and tree models are being used more and more widely in the social and biological sciences to analyze similarity relations. The purposes of this book are to describe how matrices of similarities or associations among entities can be modeled using trees and to explain some of the issues that arise in performing such analyses and correctly interpreting the results. The models discussed here include ultrametric trees (fit by the techniques widely known as "hierarchical clustering"), additive trees, and certain special cases and extensions of these basic models.

There is a need for such a book because at present many social science researchers are aware of dimensional techniques such as principal components analysis (PCA) or multidimensional scaling (MDS) for representing proximity relations but do not know when tree models might be more appropriate or how to apply these tree models. In addition, many discussions of trees in the clustering literature (e.g., Sneath & Sokal, 1973) tend to emphasize the algorithms used to fit the models rather than the interpretations of trees as *models* of proximity. Finally, much of the clustering literature has been written by statisticians or computer scientists, and consequently it has not emphasized potential applications in the social sciences.

Certain of the techniques loosely referred to as "clustering" are in fact methods for fitting tree models. Consequently, trees have been discussed to some extent in many general references on cluster analysis, such as Aldenderfer and Blashfield (1984), Hartigan (1975), Jain and Dubes (1988), and Sneath and Sokal (1973). In addition, review articles on scaling and exploratory multivariate methods that include brief sections on tree models

1

have appeared in various journals. In psychology, Shepard (1980), Carroll and Arabie (1980), Arabie and Hubert (1992), and De Soete and Carroll (in press) contain useful references. In sociology, Scott (1991) presents a history and overview of methods for social network analysis that includes some discussion of hierarchical clustering and tree models, and Hage and Harary (1983) describe applications of various types of network models in anthropology. In marketing, Punj and Stewart (1983) survey applications of clustering methods (including hierarchical methods that fit tree structures) to segment consumer populations, and DeSarbo, Manrai, and Manrai (1993) provide a comprehensive treatment of the uses of trees and related models to study consumer knowledge of products.

The material in this book is complementary to that covered in previous Sage titles on scaling and clustering. The book by Kruskal and Wish (1978) introduces multidimensional scaling methods for such data, and Arabie, Carroll, and DeSarbo (1987) present both MDS and clustering methods for three-way proximity data (e.g., data consisting of multiple proximity matrices, each from a separate "source" or subject). Aldenderfer and Blashfield (1984) present a general introduction to cluster analysis, including hierarchical clustering algorithms that are sometimes used to fit tree models. In particular, examples are given of trees produced by the algorithms known as single linkage, complete linkage, and Ward's method. The present book mentions single and complete linkage in passing but emphasizes other algorithms for fitting the tree models. This is because the goal of this book is to discuss the use of trees as *models* of proximity data and the specific ways in which aspects of the tree solution can be interpreted when applied to such data. When trees are used in such a model-fitting approach, algorithms with least squares (or maximum likelihood) properties[1] are most useful.

A second goal of this book is to make a clear distinction between ultrametric trees and additive trees, as well as discussing the conditions under which one or the other of these models might be preferable. A related issue is dealt with in the final chapter, namely the question of when tree models might be preferable to spatial geometric models, such as those fit by multidimensional scaling (MDS) or principal components analysis (PCA).

How to Use This Book

This book contains a mix of practical advice and theoretical material. The reader interested only in learning how to apply tree models to a particular research problem may wish to read selectively. Chapter 1 contains background material that relates trees to other types of models used in the social sciences and is recommended to all readers. Chapter 2 is essential. This chapter defines the two basic types of trees (ultrametric and additive) and discusses how to interpret tree solutions. Chapter 3 describes algorithms for fitting trees and may be skipped or skimmed by the reader interested only in understanding applications. Chapter 4 raises some practical issues involved in applying trees to data and describes two empirical applications. Chapter 5 is a brief summary of several proposed extensions to the basic tree models and also could be omitted by readers oriented to practical applications. Finally, Chapter 6 contains discussions of the relationship of tree models to the class of clustering methods known as partitioning and to the spatial models fit by multidimensional scaling and related techniques.

Types of Data for Scaling

Tree models can be applied to three general types of data. These types are described below using terminology adapted from the data taxonomies of Coombs (1964) and Carroll and Arabie (1980). These taxonomies are presented in more detail in Jacoby (1991).

The primary type of data to which tree structures are fit is proximity data, that is, data that can be interpreted as representing the similarity or dissimilarity of each pair of the conceptual "objects" to be scaled. The general term "proximities" is used to include both similarities (in which larger numbers represent more similar or "closer" pairs of objects) and dissimilarities (in which larger numbers represent more dissimilar or "distant" object pairs). A single matrix recording the proximity between each pair of objects is referred to as *two-way one-mode* data (Carroll & Arabie, 1980): *two-way* because the data matrix is "two-dimensional" (i.e., it has both rows and columns) and *one-mode* because both the rows and columns represent the same (single) set of entities or objects. In psychology, common examples of proximity data include ratings of the similarity of each pair of N stimuli, correlations between psychometric test items, or pairwise confusions between stimuli in a perceptual experiment. In geography, the subjective distances for pairs of locations might be studied by gathering estimates of distance or travel time. In sociology, frequency of communication or strength of friendship between pairs of individuals can be considered as measures of proximity. In marketing, applications include

4

TABLE 1.1
An Example Proximity Matrix

	Bio	Phy	Law	Pol	Ins	Car	Cab	Con
Biologist	—							
Physician	812	—						
Lawyer	727	714	—					
Police officer	156	175	195	—				
Insurance agent	123	156	162	221	—			
Carpenter	39	65	45	110	227	—		
Cab driver	52	78	39	149	188	396	—	
Construction worker	32	52	19	84	136	610	364	—

NOTE: Data are similarities among 8 occupations, derived from a sorting task (Kraus, 1976).

both "mapping" studies, in which the similarity of pairs of products is judged by consumers, and "segmentation" studies, in which the similarity of the consumers themselves to one another is analyzed. In general, any set of correlations or covariances, or measures of association (Liebetrau, 1983), between members of each pair of variables (or cases) might be analyzed as proximities. A simple example of a proximity matrix is given in Table 1.1. This table shows the similarities among 8 occupations, part of a larger matrix obtained by asking subjects to sort occupations into classes (Kraus, 1976).

Tree models also can be applied to "rectangular" matrices of preference or choice data. A rectangular matrix of preference data, for example, might be a matrix with N rows and M columns, in which the i,jth entry represents the preference of the ith observation (often a person or group of persons) for the jth stimulus. Because the preference of a person for a stimulus may be considered to be a type of proximity relation, in which liking for a stimulus is presumed to based on similarity of the stimulus to a person's "ideal," such data can be considered as *two-way two-mode* proximity data. De Soete, DeSarbo, Furnas, and Carroll (1984) describe algorithms for fitting trees to such rectangular proximity data. Table 1.2 presents an example matrix of this type, representing preference rankings of 12 described jobs by 8 subjects. Other examples of this type of data might include preference rankings of M products by N consumers in a marketing study or frequencies of association of N people with M organizations in a social network analysis.

TABLE 1.2

An Example Rectangular Proximity Data Matrix: Preference Rankings
of 12 Described Jobs by 8 Subjects

Subject	1	2	3	4	5	Described Job 6	7	8	9	10	11	12
1	4	1	12	7	2	3	8	6	5	11	9	10
2	9	12	4	8	3	10	1	11	7	2	5	6
3	11	2	1	7	6	8	3	12	9	5	4	10
4	10	5	1	12	3	6	8	11	9	4	2	7
5	7	4	2	1	8	12	5	10	6	9	3	11
6	3	8	5	6	4	11	9	7	2	12	1	10
7	7	4	6	11	5	8	1	10	3	2	12	9
8	7	3	2	9	4	11	8	6	1	10	5	12

Finally, tree models can be applied to any kind of rectangular multivariate "profile" data, in which the data matrix represents the scores of N cases or observations on M variables. This type of data arises frequently in various fields of application. For example, we could have data on $N = 136$ respondents of a survey, each having responded to $M = 20$ questionnaire items. The data matrix will then consist of 136 rows and 20 columns of numbers. In biology, a common type of data consists of N cases (individual specimens or species) measured on M characteristics. For example, the cases might be individual specimens and the measured characteristics might be some physical measurements. The cases might instead represent different species and the characteristics might be either average values of some set of physical variables or presence/absence of certain genetic information.

In marketing, one might have data on N consumers' use of M products, where the numbers are frequencies of purchase during a 1-month test period. In cluster or tree-fitting analyses of this type of multivariate profile data, the entities to be clustered and related to one another are usually the observations or cases. Note that this is in contrast to typical factor-analytic studies in the social sciences, which are used more often to investigate relationships among the variables (columns) of the multivariate profile matrix. The former type of analysis (of cases) is sometimes termed a Q-mode analysis, whereas the latter (analysis of variables) is referred to as an R-mode analysis (Sneath & Sokal, 1973).

Most applications of tree models to multivariate profile data begin with the data analyst selecting some similarity or association coefficient (for example, correlation or Euclidean distance) that is used to define the proximity between the members of each pair of row objects (cases) of the matrix (Aldenderfer & Blashfield, 1984; Hartigan, 1975).[2] Completion of this step results in an $N \times N$ proximity matrix. Because this matrix generally is symmetric, it can be represented either as a square symmetric matrix or as a lower-half matrix with $(N)(N-1)/2$ entries. On the other hand, note that if one is interested instead in investigating relationships among column entities, as in a typical factor-analytic study, it is also possible to use the proximity coefficient to define the proximity between each pair of *columns,* resulting in an $M \times M$ matrix of proximities among "variables" or items. Once the proximities among the row (or column) objects are calculated, any of the methods described in this book for fitting trees to square symmetric proximity matrices can be employed to analyze the similarity relations among the objects of interest.

Types of Models of Proximity Relations

There are four important types of models that have been applied to proximity data in social science applications. These types are spatial/dimensional, cluster, set-theoretic, and graph-theoretic models. Each of these is described below, and the relationship of trees to that general type of model is explained.

Spatial/Dimensional Models

Dimensional models, including metric and nonmetric multidimensional scaling (MDS), principal components analysis (PCA) and factor analysis (FA), and correspondence analysis, have been used widely in the social sciences. These models represent the proximities among objects by locating the objects as points in a low-dimensional geometric space. In MDS, distances between points in the derived space can be considered to be modeling the original (data) dissimilarities. In the case of metric MDS (Torgerson, 1958), this modeling relationship between the derived model distances and the original proximity data is required to be a linear function; for nonmetric MDS, this relationship is merely required to be monotonic (see Kruskal & Wish, 1978).

Trees constitute an alternative to spatial/dimensional models and may fit different aspects of a data set from those found by a spatial model (Carroll, 1976; Pruzansky, Tversky, & Carroll, 1982; Sattath & Tversky, 1977). In Chapter 6, the relationship between spaces and trees is discussed in some detail, along with some suggestions as to how a user might decide whether spatial or tree models are more appropriate for a given set of proximity data.

Cluster Models

For present purposes, clustering methods can be grouped into three classes according to the type of model they fit to the proximity data. The classes are *partitioning methods, hierarchical clustering,* and *overlapping nonhierarchical clustering.* The common purpose of all these methods is to group objects into sets or clusters, such that each cluster contains relatively similar objects.

Partitioning methods are designed to find a set of clusters that correspond to mutually exclusive and exhaustive subsets of the set of objects being analyzed. In a partition, each object is a member of exactly one cluster. *Hierarchical methods* find sets of clusters that are restricted to be nested; that is, either each pair of clusters must be disjoint (i.e., have no objects in common) or one cluster must be included in the other (i.e., the objects composing one cluster are a subset of the items in the other cluster) (Carroll & Corter, 1995). The nested set of clusters resulting from a hierarchical clustering method can be represented by a tree graph, or "dendrogram." Finally, *overlapping nonhierarchical clustering methods* fit sets of clusters that are not necessarily restricted to this hierarchical or nested relationship; instead, the clusters may overlap in arbitrary patterns. These three classes of clustering models are mentioned in increasing order of complexity and generality: A partition is a special case of a hierarchical clustering solution, which is a special case of an overlapping nonhierarchical clustering.

Ultrametric trees (defined in Chapter 2) are a type of hierarchical clustering model that may be fit by simple agglomerative algorithms, such as single-, complete-, or average-link clustering (Aldenderfer & Blashfield, 1984; Sneath & Sokal, 1973). Additive trees (Chapter 2) are not fit by any of these commonly used clustering algorithms and bear a less direct relationship to simple cluster models. An additive tree displayed in rooted form (see Chapter 2), however, may also be thought of as a type of hierarchical clustering model.

Set-Theoretic Models

Tversky (1977) presented a mathematical model of similarity relations, termed the *contrast* or "feature-matching" model. The contrast model analyzes the similarity between two objects as a function of the number and salience of the discrete features shared by the objects (their "common features") and the number and salience of features that each object has that the other does not. The contrast model expresses the dissimilarity between two objects x and y as

$$d(x, y) = -\Theta g\,(X \cap Y) + \alpha f(X - Y) + \beta f(Y - X) \qquad (1.1)$$

where X and Y represent the feature sets associated with objects x and y respectively, and α and β are nonnegative weights. The set functions g and f define the saliences or weights of individual features and how they are combined to yield the overall contributions of the three relevant feature sets. These sets are $X \cap Y$, which denotes the common features of X and Y; $X - Y$, which denotes the distinctive features of x (with respect to y); and $Y - X$, which denotes the distinctive features of y.

Various special cases of the contrast model are interesting in their own right. For example, setting $\alpha = \beta = 0$ and assuming that the function g is additive leads to a simple *common-features model* in which the similarity of x and y is given by the sum of the weights of their common features. Alternatively, setting $\alpha = \beta$ and $\Theta = 0$ (and assuming f additive) results in the additive symmetric *distinctive-features model* (Restle, 1959; Tversky, 1977). These two special cases will be useful in interpreting certain aspects of tree solutions, as discussed in Chapter 2.

Graph-Theoretic Models

In sociology, there has been a tradition of representing networks of social relations using graphs (e.g., Scott, 1991). In addition, the psychometric and clustering literatures recently have seen an upsurge of interest in modeling proximity relations using graphs and directed graphs (e.g., Hutchinson, 1989; Klauer, 1989; Klauer & Carroll, 1989; Schvaneveld, 1990). In a typical graph representation of proximities among N objects, each object is represented as a point or "node" of the graph. Proximity relations are represented by arcs or lines that connect these nodes. In the general case of a graph, any pair of nodes in the graph may be connected by an arc. The proximity between two objects is usually modeled by the distance, defined as the length of the minimum-length path between the two corresponding nodes. In a typical application that seeks to model a set of proximities by a graph, both the set of arcs that are defined between pairs of nodes and the weight of each arc are parameters to be estimated.

Trees are a special type of graph model. In the graph-theoretic literature, "tree" has a very specific meaning. A *tree* graph is defined as a connected

9

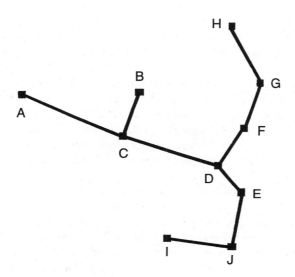

Figure 1.1. Minimal Spanning Tree on 10 Points in the Plane

graph without cycles. (A cycle is a path consisting of more than two arcs that leads from a particular node back to itself, passing through no node more than once.) As with more general types of graphs, tree graphs may be *directed* (with a direction assigned to each arc) or *undirected* (no directionality to arcs). Figure 1.1 represents a tree graph defined on ten nodes representing ten objects. It can be seen that the graph is connected (i.e., a path can be found to link any pair of nodes) and that the graph contains no cycles. Note that no additional arcs can be added to the graph in Figure 1.1 without creating a cycle, so that the graph would no longer be a tree. For example, if an arc were added to link nodes A and B, then a cycle of length 3 would be created (linking points A, B, and C). If an arc were added linking points B and H, a cycle of length 6 would be created, and again the graph would no longer be a tree.

In fact, the graph in Figure 1.1 is a special tree, termed the *minimal spanning tree,* for these points. The minimal spanning tree is defined as the tree graph of minimal length that connects ("spans") all the nodes of the graph, where the length of a tree is defined as the sum of the lengths of all the arcs in the graph. A minimal spanning tree always has exactly $N - 1$ arcs, where N is the number of nodes or objects. Furthermore, note that each node in this tree corresponds to one of the objects being modeled. Given data consisting of the proximities among a set of N objects, the minimal spanning tree can be found easily by any of several algorithms (e.g., Kruskal, 1956).

Minimal spanning trees have been discussed in the clustering and graph-theoretic literature, and they have important applications in designing efficient transportation or communication networks. Minimal spanning trees, however, rarely have been used as models for social science data. In part, that is because a minimal spanning tree algorithm does not achieve two goals that generally are considered important in such work: It does not tend to find highly homogeneous clusters of objects, and it does not find the tree that can best reproduce the proximities among the objects. Another important difference between the spanning tree and the types of tree models discussed in this book is that in a spanning tree, an object may be represented either by an internal node of the tree or by an external or "leaf" node.[3] In contrast, the ultrametric tree and additive tree models that are introduced in the following chapter have the following characteristics. First, it is usually assumed that the objects on which the proximities are defined are to be represented in the tree graph only by external nodes ("leaves") of the tree graph, and not by internal nodes (but see Carroll, 1976). Therefore, internal nodes in these types of trees usually can be interpreted as corresponding to clusters of objects. Second, it is commonly assumed that the goal of the analysis is to find a tree structure that accurately models the proximity data, in the sense that the path-length distances in the tree are as close as possible (in a least squares sense) to the original proximities.

NOTES

1. Saying that a tree-fitting algorithm has "least squares" properties means that the parameters of the tree model, namely the structure of the tree and the lengths of arcs in the tree graph, are chosen so that distances between pairs of objects in the tree, $\hat{d}_{ij}$, reproduce as closely as possible the observed (data) dissimilarities, d_{ij}. Specifically, the parameter values chosen are the values that minimize the sum of squared differences between each model (tree) distance and its corresponding observed dissimilarity.

2. Note, however, that certain hierarchical clustering algorithms (e.g., Ward, 1963) cluster cases by operating directly on multivariate data of this type.

3. The following standard terminology will be used to describe the nodes and arcs of a tree. An "external" (or "leaf") node of a tree is a node of degree one, that is, a node with only a single arc leading from it. An "internal" node has two or more (but usually three) arcs leading from it.

2. TWO TYPES OF TREE MODELS

Ultrametric Trees

As an introductory example of an ultrametric tree applied to model a simple proximity matrix, Figure 2.1a shows a matrix representing hypothetical judgments of dissimilarity among five crimes: arson, burglary, perjury, shoplifting, and vandalism (this example is suggested by a study conducted by Howe, 1988). Figure 2.1b shows the representation of the data as an ultrametric tree. This example will be discussed in more detail below, but for now notice that the tree organizes highly similar crimes (e.g., *burglary* and *shoplifting*) into the same branch of the tree. Conversely, relatively dissimilar crimes (e.g., *perjury* and *arson*) are relatively distant in the tree. Some of the higher branches in the tree are labeled as well (e.g., "stealing"). These labels do not result directly from the analysis but merely reflect interpretations of aspects of the tree structure made by the researcher.

Mathematically, an ultrametric tree can be characterized in the following way. The path-length distances between objects in an ultrametric tree satisfy the following mathematical relationship, known as the *ultrametric inequality*. This inequality states that for any three objects a, b, and c in the tree,

$$\hat{d}(a, b) \le \mathrm{MAX}[\hat{d}(a, c), \hat{d}(b, c)]. \tag{2.1}$$

This inequality holds under all possible relabelings of the three points as a, b, and c. Alternatively, the ultrametric inequality can be expressed as stating that for every triple of objects, there exists one labeling of the objects x, y, and z such that:

$$\hat{d}(x, y) \le \hat{d}(x, z) = \hat{d}(y, z). \tag{2.2}$$

This way of stating the ultrametric inequality makes plain the correspondence of the terms in the inequality to the actual tree graph representing the proximities, as follows. For any three objects x, y, and z for which Equation 2.2 is true (and the inequality is strict), x and y are less distant from each other than either is from z. This implies that x and y form a subtree (cluster) relative to z. For example, in Figure 2.1b it can be seen that the crimes of *burglary* (*bu*) and *shoplifting* (*sh*) form a subtree when compared to *arson* (*ar*). In the proximity matrix shown in Figure 2.1a,

12

a. Dissimilarities

	Ar	Bu	Pe	Sh	Va
Arson	--				
Burglary	8	--			
Perjury	10	10	--		
Shoplifting	8	2	10	--	
Vandalism	4	8	10	8	--

b. Ultrametric Tree

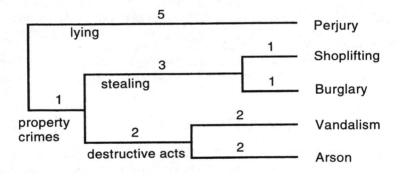

Figure 2.1. Ultrametric Tree of Hypothetical Dissimilarities Among Crimes

$$d(bu, sh) \leq d(bu, ar) = d(sh, ar)$$

$$2 \leq 8 = 8 . \tag{2.3}$$

It can be verified easily from the proximity matrix that the three distances among the objects in every triple satisfy the ultrametric inequality. In fact, these proximities have been made up specifically to be fit perfectly by an ultrametric tree. In this context, "perfect fit" means that the path-length distances in the tree between the "leaves" corresponding to every pair of objects x and y are linearly related to $d(x, y)$, the observed dissimilarities between the objects. Stated another way, the path-length distances in the tree and the observed dissimilarities have a correlation of 1. In fact, for this particular example the "model distances" (i.e., the path lengths in the tree) and the observed proximities are identical, as can be verified easily by referring to the lengths listed below each arc. For example, the observed dissimilarity between *arson* and *perjury*, $d(ar, pe)$, is 10, and the path length between them is given by the sum of the arc lengths along the path connecting them, $\hat{d}(ar, pe) = 2 + 2 + 1 + 5 = 10$. It should be noted that the vertical lines in Figure 2.1b are not taken into account in calculating the path-length distances; they merely serve to connect the (meaningful) horizontal arcs.

One special case of the mathematical relationship described by the ultrametric inequality corresponds to a special (degenerate) case of the tree graph. Specifically, if $\hat{d}(x, y) = \hat{d}(x, z) = \hat{d}(y, z)$, then the three objects all "join" at a single internal node. For example, assume that an additional crime, *purse snatching*, had been included in the set of crimes to be rated and that the three pairwise dissimilarities among *purse snatching, shoplifting,* and *burglary* were all equal to 2. Then *purse snatching* would appear on a third leaf emanating from the node below the "stealing" arc, and this node would have a total of four arcs emanating from it (one "parent" and three "children").

Unlike the artificial data of Figure 2.1a, most empirically derived data will not exactly satisfy the ultrametric inequality for every triple of dissimilarities. The consequence is that the data cannot be represented perfectly by an ultrametric tree. One potential reason that real data might not everywhere satisfy the ultrametric inequality is measurement error or "noise" in the data. In this (common) case, it seems appropriate to ignore the minor violations and to use a clustering procedure that attempts to find the "best-fitting" ultrametric tree (such as the algorithms described in Chapter 3).

Alternatively, the data might violate the ultrametric inequality in certain *systematic* ways, suggesting that a more general model (e.g., an additive tree) might be more appropriate for the application. This situation is not uncommon, because the ultrametric inequality imposes very strict constraints on proximity data. As an example, consider the frequencies of communications among several workers, designated as A, B, and C. For this hypothetical example, directionality of messages is disregarded. Therefore, any message, whether from A to B or from B to A, is counted as a communication between them. Assume that A and B share an office, so that they communicate more often with each other than with other workers, whereas C is in a different office. A sends 15 messages per day to any worker with whom he shares an office and 10 messages to any worker not in his office (such as C). C has the same pattern. Assume that B, however, is much less communicative and sends only 10 messages to any worker with whom he shares an office and 5 to any other worker. This results in the (bidirectional) communication frequencies $s(A, B) = 15 + 10 = 25$, $s(A, C) = 10 + 10 = 20$, and $s(B, C) = 5 + 10 = 15$, where $s(A, B) = 25$ means that workers A and B send 25 messages back and forth per day. These communication frequencies can be considered to be measures of association or "closeness" of the pairs. Typically, such similarities are converted to dissimilarities before applying a tree-fitting algorithm, by subtracting each of the similarities from a sufficiently large constant so that all resulting dissimilarities are nonnegative. Using a constant of 40, the resulting dissimilarities are $d(A, B) = 15$, $d(A, C) = 20$, and $d(B, C) = 25$. This plausible pattern of communication frequencies can be seen to violate the ultrametric inequality, because the two larger dissimilarities representing "interoffice" communication ought to be equal but are not: $d(A, B) < d(A, C) \neq d(B, C)$. These dissimilarities therefore cannot be represented by an ultrametric tree. In a tree, if A and B join together to form a cluster (i.e., they are each other's nearest neighbor), they are restricted by the ultrametric inequality to be equally dissimilar to any other worker not in the cluster. Obviously, this is an extremely restrictive condition, not likely to be satisfied by real data. In such cases, the ultrametric tree might not be an appropriate model for the data, and the researcher might want to consider a less restrictive model such as the additive tree model discussed in a later section.

Common-Features Interpretation of Ultrametric Trees

Besides the general structure of the tree, which shows the pairs of entities that are highly similar and the ones that are less so, other aspects of an ultrametric model are also interpretable. In particular, the lengths of arcs in the tree graph are meaningful. One way of interpreting these lengths is provided by Tversky's (1977) feature-matching model of similarity. Under a common-features interpretation, the length of each arc in the rooted tree is a measure of the importance of the set of features shared by all the objects in that branch (subtree) of the tree. For example, in Figure 2.1b, *arson* (*ar*) and *vandalism* (*va*) join at a common "ancestor" node, which is labeled "destructive acts" (this interpretation is made purely on theoretical grounds and is not based on any aspect of the data or statistical information). This node is joined by an arc of length 2 to its immediate ancestor, which is a node labeled "property crimes" that combines the "destructive acts" cluster with that labeled "stealing." The interpretation of the length of this arc is that the set of features or properties shared by *arson* and *vandalism* (but not by any other objects in the set) have weight or salience 2. Similarly, the fact that the arc labeled "stealing" has length 3 indicates that the features shared by *burglary* and *shoplifting* (but not by any other objects) have total weight 3. Finally, the arc corresponding to the "property crimes" cluster, with length 1, indicates that all four crimes against property share features with weight 1. Thus the total weight of the features or properties shared by *arson* (*ar*) and *vandalism* (*va*) can be measured as $1 + 2 = 3$, the sum of the arc lengths on the path from the root of the tree to the node where *ar* and *va* first join. These shared properties are known as the "common features" of *arson* and *vandalism* (Tversky, 1977).

To summarize, an ultrametric tree can be interpreted as a graphical representation of an additive common-features model of proximity, in which the feature sets are restricted to have a hierarchical or nested structure (corresponding to the clusters determined by the tree structure) (Corter & Tversky, 1986; Sattath & Tversky, 1977). The weight or measure of the common features of two objects, x and y, is represented in the graph by the sum of the arc lengths leading from the root of the tree to the lowest[1] node that is an "ancestor" of both x and y (sometimes referred to as the "least common ancestor" node for x and y). The length of the arc leading from this least common ancestor node to its immediate parent represents the weight of the features shared by all (and *only*) those objects "under" this node.

The dendrograms (tree diagrams) drawn by the clustering routines of statistical packages often represent interobject dissimilarities by a convention different from the path-length convention presented above. For example, algorithms for "single-link" or "minimum-method" hierarchical clustering begin by selecting the two objects x and y with the lowest dissimilarity value to be combined into the first cluster, C_{xy}. The value of the dissimilarity between them, $d(x, y)$, commonly is used as the height of the cluster in the dendrogram. The distance from this new cluster to any other object z in the set is then defined as the smaller of the dissimilarities $d(x, z)$ and $d(y, z)$:

$$d(C_{xy}, z) = \text{MIN}[d(x, z), d(y, z)]. \qquad (2.4)$$

The rows (and columns) of the proximity matrix corresponding to x and y are then replaced with a single row and column corresponding to cluster C_{xy}. This new reduced proximity matrix is then searched for a minimal value corresponding to the least dissimilar pair of objects/clusters. When this minimal dissimilarity is found, it becomes the height of the new cluster formed, and so forth. In this type of dendrogram, the dissimilarity between any two objects is read off not as the path length between the two objects but as the height of the "lowest" node (cluster) of which the two objects are both members (i.e., their "least common ancestor" node). This convention for representing distances in an ultrametric tree can be termed the "node-height" convention, in contrast to the "path-length" convention used in this book. These conventions are equivalent in the sense that any proximity matrix that can be represented by a node-height tree also can be represented by a path-length tree, and vice versa (Carroll & Corter, 1995).

The node-height convention for representing distances in an ultrametric tree makes the parsimony of the model especially apparent, because it makes clear that only $N - 1$ real-valued parameters must be estimated. These parameters correspond to the heights of the $N - 1$ higher-order nodes that are formed in clustering N objects in this pairwise agglomerative fashion. This parsimony is related to the restrictiveness of the ultrametric inequality: With fewer parameters, a model has fewer ways to accommodate meaningful variance in the data.

Additive Trees

The additive tree is a less restrictive model than the ultrametric tree. A simple example of an additive tree and the artificial proximity data that generated it are given in Figure 2.2. This set of hypothetical dissimilarities is based on the previously introduced example of communication patterns among workers.

In the same way that the ultrametric inequality states the basic mathematical relationship characterizing distances in an ultrametric tree, so there is a mathematical relationship that characterizes distances among objects in an additive tree (Buneman, 1971; Dobson, 1974). This relationship, known as the additive or tree inequality, states that distances in an additive tree among any four objects a, b, c, and d satisfy the following relationship:

$$\hat{d}(a, b) + \hat{d}(c, d) \leq \text{MAX}[\hat{d}(a, c) + \hat{d}(b, d), \hat{d}(b, c) + \hat{d}(a, d)]. \quad (2.5)$$

a. Dissimiliarities

	A	B	C	D	E
Worker A	--				
Worker B	15	--			
Worker C	20	25	--		
Worker D	18	23	6	--	
Worker E	20	25	20	18	--

b. Additive Tree

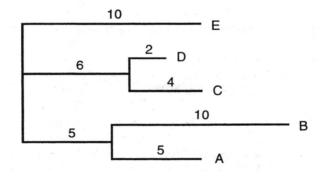

Figure 2.2. Additive Tree of Hypothetical Worker Communication Patterns

The above relationship is true no matter how the four objects are labeled *a*, *b*, *c*, and *d*. An alternative way of expressing the additive inequality is to note that it requires that any four objects in the tree have some relabeling *x*, *y*, *u*, and *v* such that:

$$\hat{d}(x, y) + \hat{d}(u, v) \le \hat{d}(x, u) + \hat{d}(y, v) = \hat{d}(x, v) + \hat{d}(y, u) . \qquad (2.6)$$

This way of stating the additive inequality makes clearer the relationship between the mathematical statement and the actual tree structure: The particular pattern of dissimilarities described in Equation 2.6 corresponds to the tree shown in Figure 2.3, in which *x* and *y* are "neighbors," as are *u*

18

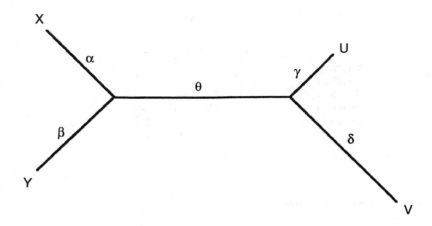

Figure 2.3. An Unrooted Additive Tree on Four Objects

and v. Note that the simple additive tree portrayed in Figure 2.3 is displayed in "unrooted" form, while that of Figure 2.2b is rooted (i.e., one point in the tree graph has been chosen to be portrayed at the "top," with all arcs descending from this point). More will be said about this later.

It is not hard to verify that the dissimilarities among every quadruple of objects in the data of Figure 2.2a satisfy the additive inequality. There are exactly five quadruples of objects for which the additive inequality must be checked: *A-B-C-D*, *A-B-C-E*, *A-B-D-E*, *A-C-D-E*, and *B-C-D-E*. For example,

$$d(A, B) + d(C, D) < d(A, C) + d(B, D) = d(A, D) + d(B, C)$$

$$21 < 43 = 43 . \tag{2.7}$$

The relationship also is satisfied for the other four quadruples. For real data, this relationship usually will not be satisfied for all quadruples because of error. The path-length distances in the tree itself (the "model distances"), however, always satisfy the additive inequality, because that is the defining characteristic of distances in an additive tree.

The constraints imposed on the proximities by the additive inequality (Equation 2.6) are less severe than for the ultrametric (Equation 2.2). This can be demonstrated easily by considering the patterns of communication among workers *A*, *B*, and *C*, as described above. As already explained, the pattern of communication frequencies among workers *A*, *B*, and *C* could not be represented by an ultrametric tree because the corresponding distances did not satisfy the ultrametric inequality. This pattern *can* be represented by the additive tree of Figure 2.2b, as can be verified easily by calculating path-length distances among the three leaves labeled *A*, *B*, and *C*. These path-length distances are $\hat{d}(A, B) = 15$, $\hat{d}(A, C) = 20$, and $\hat{d}(B, C) = 25$, identical to the observed dissimilarities in Figure 2.2a. That some patterns of proximities can be represented by an additive tree but not by an ultrametric tree illustrates that the ultrametric tree is a special case of an additive tree.

Perhaps the most obvious difference between ultrametric trees and additive trees is that the lengths of leaf arcs in an additive tree are free to be of any (nonnegative) length. Put another way, in an ultrametric tree all leaf nodes are equally distant from the root of the tree, but in an additive tree these distances may be unequal. This again underscores that the additive tree model is more general than the ultrametric: If all leaves in a rooted additive tree were constrained to be equidistant from the root, an ultrametric tree would result (i.e., distances in the tree would satisfy the ultrametric inequality).

An additive tree is a very general structure. Many other structures can be seen to be special cases of the additive tree. One of these special cases corresponds to a special case of the additive inequality, Equation 2.6. Specifically, if equality holds among the three sums,

$$\hat{d}(A, B) + \hat{d}(C, D) = \hat{d}(A, C) + \hat{d}(B, D) = \hat{d}(A, D) + \hat{d}(B, C) \qquad (2.8)$$

then the additive tree connecting these points will be a *singular tree* with a single internal node (sometimes called a "bush" or "star") (Figure 2.4a). As is apparent from the figure, in this degenerate case of the additive tree, each of the leaf arcs may have different lengths. Another special case of the additive tree is a (one-dimensional) line (Figure 2.4b).

Additive trees may be represented either in rooted or in unrooted form. Figure 2.5a shows an additive tree displayed in unrooted form; Figure 2.5b shows the corresponding tree portrayed in rooted form. The path-length distances in the tree are not affected by this change of the manner in which the tree is displayed, but the most natural type of feature interpretation of the tree does differ for the two structures. As discussed in the next section, an unrooted additive tree is naturally interpreted in terms of the distinctive

20

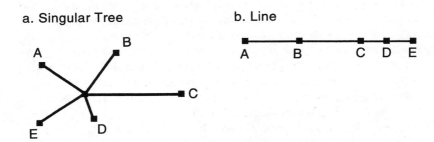

a. Singular Tree

A

B

C

E   D

b. Line

A   B   C D E

Figure 2.4. Two Special Cases of the Additive Tree

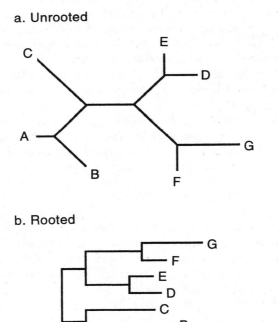

a. Unrooted

C

E

D

A

B

F

G

b. Rooted

G

F

E

D

C

B

A

Figure 2.5. An Additive Tree Displayed in Unrooted and Rooted Forms

features of objects, while a rooted additive tree has a natural interpretation in terms of common features of sets of objects, plus the unique features of each single object. The *unique features* for object x, for example, are those properties or attributes possessed only by object x (and by no other object).

Choosing a Root for an Additive Tree

The specific interpretation of the tree in terms of feature sets can be affected not only by whether the tree is displayed in rooted versus unrooted form but also by where in the tree the root is placed. In an ultrametric tree, there is a unique point in the tree that is equidistant from all the leaf nodes; this is the root. An additive tree, however, may be rooted at any point in the tree graph. Consequently, a single (unrooted) additive tree corresponds to an infinite number of rooted additive trees, because the root may be placed arbitrarily at any point in the tree graph. As discussed later, the exact rooting selected can determine how arcs are interpreted as representing either common features or distinctive features of objects.

There is an even more basic way in which the placement of a root can affect a researcher's conclusions about the domain, especially if the unwary researcher does not realize that the placement of the root is arbitrary. Note that if the root is placed along any arc in the tree, there will in general be exactly two clusters distinguished by the root, that is, two subtrees that descend from the root. If, however, the root is placed exactly at an internal node (which is usually of degree three), there will be three subtrees that descend from the root, corresponding to three major clusters of objects. Sometimes researchers may make a statement such as "Three major clusters of objects were found by the algorithm," without considering that another placement of the root might result in a division into only two clusters. If certain arcs in the tree have length 0, then there may be internal nodes that are of degree four or more. Rooting the tree at such an internal node would result in a high-level division of the objects into four or more clusters or groups.

The choice of a root therefore is a decision that ought to be made carefully by the researcher. The problem of rooting the additive tree may seem reminiscent of the rotation problem of factor analysis, in which a given factor structure can be rotated into any of an infinite number of structures that all fit the data equally well but that lead to quite different interpretations. Consequently, researchers using additive trees ought to be alert to potential alternate rootings that might provide differing perspectives on the data.

If theoretical or substantive considerations offer a guide, perhaps the best solution to the rooting problem is to select the root so as to enhance interpretability. Some researchers, however, may desire a more objective way of selecting the root. In addition, in exploratory applications theory may not be well enough developed to aid in selecting a root. In such cases, it may be best to have the root selected automatically by the program fitting the tree to data. To do this in a principled way, it would be desirable to have some sort of objective statistical criterion for selecting a root. Fit of the model (as measured by the sum of squared errors, or by the squared correlation, R^2, of the model distances to the proximities) does not serve as a useful statistical criterion in selecting among potential roots because (as previously noted) the distances in an additive tree are not affected by the choice of root.

One proposed objective method for choosing a root is to pick the root that minimizes the variance of the distances of the individual leaves to the root (Sattath & Tversky, 1977). Use of this criterion to pick a rooting tends to create "balanced" trees, that is, trees that have an approximately equal number of objects on each of the subtrees descending from the root. This criterion also tends to create tree displays that correspond closely to the displays of ultrametric trees of the same data (because in an ultrametric tree, this variance of the distances from the root to the leaves is not merely minimized, it is necessarily equal to zero). A simpler way of automatically selecting the root is available if a sequential agglomerative clustering algorithm (such as those used to fit ultrametric trees) is used to construct the additive tree. Such algorithms combine objects or groups in a stepwise fashion, with the root being placed by default on the arc joining the nodes representing the last two (or three) objects or groups to be combined. This simple default method of picking the root usually gives satisfactory results.

Feature Interpretations of Additive Trees

An unrooted tree can be thought of as graphically representing the distinctive features of sets of objects (Sattath & Tversky, 1977; Tversky, 1977). The distinctive features of an object x (relative to y) consist of the features or attributes that are associated with x but not with y; similarly, the distinctive features of y (relative to x) are those features of y that are not shared by x. More formally, the distinctive features of x and y can be denoted as $X \Delta Y = (X - Y) \cup (Y - X)$, where $\cup$ denotes set union and $-$ denotes set difference. In the unrooted tree, the arc joining two objects (or sets of objects) x and y represents the summed weights of the distinctive features of x and y. For example, in Figure 2.5a, there is a central arc that, if deleted, would form two subtrees: one containing objects A, B, and C and the other containing objects D, E, F, and G. The length of this arc represents the summed weights of the distinctive features of the two sets $\{A, B, C\}$ and $\{D, E, F, G\}$, that is, the features that A, B, and C share but that D, E, F, and G do not have and the features that D, E, F, and G share that A, B, and C do not. The tree does not give any information about the comparative importance or weight of the distinctive features of the set $\{A, B, C\}$ relative to the weight of the distinctive features of $\{D, E, F, G\}$. This ambiguity extends even to the lengths of leaf arcs. For example, the leaf arc corresponding to object C may be thought of as reflecting both the unique features of C (that is, the features or attributes that C alone has) and the features that characterize all the objects in the tree except C. In fact, the length of the leaf arc reflects the summed weights of both types of features.[2]

As noted earlier, a rooted *ultrametric* tree can be interpreted as representing a common-features model of similarity (Tversky, 1977). A rooted additive tree, in contrast, can be interpreted as representing both patterns of common features shared by objects *and* the unique features of individual objects (Sattath & Tversky, 1977; see also Carroll, 1976). For example, in Figure 2.5b the fact that the leaf arc for object B is longer than the leaf arc for object A indicates that object B has relatively more unique features (i.e., features not shared by any other object) than does object A. Interpreting the arcs of a rooted additive tree in this way requires mentally "cutting" the tree vertically, dividing it into an ultrametric tree plus N single arcs, each corresponding to one of the objects being scaled. Figure 2.6 illustrates how a rooted additive tree can be divided in this way. The resulting ultrametric tree (Figure 2.6b) is then interpreted in terms of common features, while the lengths of the leaf arcs in the singular tree (Figure 2.6b) are interpreted as representing the importance of the unique features of each object.

Another example can be used to illustrate several points about displaying additive trees in rooted form. First, note that this decomposition of path lengths in an additive tree into a set of ultrametric distances plus distances generated by a singular tree is not unique (Carroll & Corter, 1995). For example, in Figure 2.7a it can be seen that increasing the length of the branch corresponding to objects A, B, and C while decreasing the length of the branch for D, E, F, and G by the same amount before slicing the tree into ultrametric and singular tree components would result in ultrametric/singular trees with different arc lengths. Both decompositions, however, perfectly re-create the additive tree distances.

24

a. Additive Tree

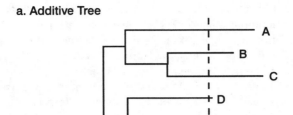

b. Ultrametric Tree + Singular Tree

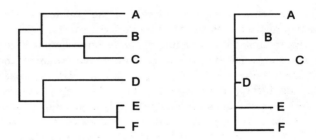

Figure 2.6. Decomposition of an Additive Tree Into the Sum of an Ultrametric and a Singular Tree

The additive tree of Figure 2.7 also can be used to illustrate how changing the root can change not only the relative weights of certain sets of common and unique features but even whether certain sets of common features are thought to be present. For example, the rooted tree of Figure 2.7a suggests that there are two main clusters of objects, $\{A, B, C\}$ and $\{D, E, F, G\}$, each having roughly equally salient sets of common features. The re-rooting illustrated in Figure 2.7b indicates how this interpretation might change if this tree were re-rooted so that the root were placed exactly at the internal node where objects A, B, and C join. This re-rooting operation can be visualized by imagining that the horizontal lines in the graph are

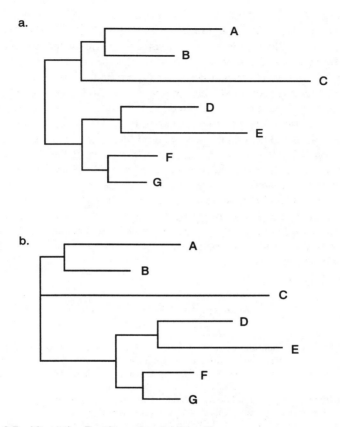

Figure 2.7. Alternative Rootings of an Additive Tree

made of rigid sticks, that the vertical connector lines are elastic, and that the graph is "picked up" at the point corresponding to the new root. The result is a new rooted tree (shown in Figure 2.7b) in which there are now three main clusters, one containing objects A and B, one containing only C, and one containing $\{D, E, F, G\}$. The arc leading from the root to the node corresponding to the set $\{D, E, F, G\}$ will be much longer than in the original tree of Figure 2.7a; in fact, the length of this arc will be equal to the sum of the two arcs in the old tree corresponding to the sets $\{A, B, C\}$ and $\{D, E, F, G\}$. It can be seen that the new rooting suggests a new interpretation of this arc as corresponding entirely to common features of

{D, E, F, G} (in contrast to the original interpretation of this arc as representing in part the common features of {A, B, C}). These examples provide further illustration of the point made previously, that the choice of a root for an additive tree, though arbitrary from the standpoint of how well the model fits the data, can affect the interpretation of the results.

Other aspects of a rooted additive tree graph also are interpretable. For example, the closeness of a leaf node to the root gives a visual index of how typical the corresponding object is (i.e., how similar to all other objects) relative to the other objects in its subtree (i.e., relative to the other objects on the same branch leading from the root). If the root has been chosen in some "rational" way (e.g., using the minimum variance criterion), then it is reasonable to interpret the closeness of the object to the root as indicating typicality relative to all the objects being scaled. For example, object C of Figure 2.7a is the most distant from the root; therefore, this object can be considered to be the least typical object of the set. Objects B, F, and G are all relatively close to the root; therefore, these objects can be seen to be the most typical.

NOTES

1. It is conventional to discuss rooted trees as if they were oriented with the root at the top and the "leaves" at the bottom. For example, nodes that are relatively close to the root are said to be "high" in the tree, while nodes that are close to the leaves are said to be "low."

2. It could be argued that features shared by all objects in the set except A will be relatively rare or unimportant compared to features of A that are unique to A. The length of this arc therefore is likely to reflect mainly the importance of unique features of A.

3. ALGORITHMS FOR FITTING TREES TO DATA

Proximities Among N Objects (2-way 1-mode data)

Ultrametric Trees

As described in Chapter 1, an ultrametric tree can be constructed by any of several commonly used methods for sequential agglomerative clustering, such as single-link, complete-link, or average-link clustering (Aldenderfer & Blashfield, 1984; Sneath & Sokal, 1973). In the psychometric literature, these techniques are usually associated with Johnson's (1967) article, which described the single- and complete-link algorithms.

Although the procedures mentioned above can be used to construct an ultrametric tree and usually work well in practice, they are not guaranteed to find the optimal (in a least squares sense) tree structure for the given proximity matrix. The optimal tree in a least squares sense is the tree for which the interobject path-length distances reproduce as well as possible the matrix of proximities; that is, it is a tree for which the sum of squared errors

$$\text{SSE} = \Sigma \, [d(x, y) - \hat{d}(x, y)]^2 \tag{3.1}$$

is minimal, where $d(x, y)$ represents the data dissimilarity between objects x and y and $\hat{d}(x, y)$ represents the tree (model) distance between them. Several algorithms have been proposed that explicitly attempt to find the least squares tree. Hartigan (1967) first considered the fit of a matrix of model (tree) distances to a matrix of data dissimilarities possibly containing error, proposing a heuristic combinatorial algorithm that attempted to maximize the fit of the ultrametric tree to the data (i.e., to find a least squares solution). Carroll and Pruzansky (1975) described a mathematical programming approach (see Appendix A) to this problem that, under certain conditions, can be guaranteed to find the optimal solution. De Soete (1984b) continued this work, investigating the effectiveness of the algorithm and extending it to accommodate the more difficult problem of fitting a tree to incomplete data (De Soete, 1984c).

The Carroll-Pruzansky-De Soete algorithm for fitting ultrametric trees works as follows. First, if the input data are similarities (i.e., a larger number indicates more similarity), the data are transformed into dissimilarities by subtracting them from a sufficiently large constant. The resulting dissimilarities are further transformed if necessary to satisfy the axioms of a metric space: symmetry (i.e., $d(x, y) = d(y, x)$), positivity ($d(x, y) > d(x, x) = 0$), and the triangle inequality ($d(x, y) + d(y, z) \geq d(x, z)$ for all x, y, and z). Symmetry usually is achieved by averaging corresponding entries in the upper and lower halves of the matrix, while positivity and the triangle inequality can be satisfied by adding a sufficiently large constant to all the dissimilarities. The resulting matrix of transformed data values, interpretable as distances, can be designated D^T.

The logic of the algorithm is based on the fact that an ultrametric tree representation of the data exists if and only if the data satisfy the ultrametric inequality in Equation 2.2 (Hartigan, 1967). Accordingly, the transformed data matrix D^T is iteratively adjusted, using a technique known as *gradient descent,* in order to improve the value of a criterion measure. The criterion measure used is actually a "badness-of-fit" measure, so that the goal of the algorithm is to find the matrix that *minimizes* the measure. The particular criterion measure chosen has two parts to it: The first part measures how poorly the adjusted matrix corresponds to the original (transformed) data matrix (using the SSE criterion described above), and the second part measures if and how badly the adjusted matrix violates the ultrametric inequality (Equation 2.2). The algorithm seeks to minimize the value of this "badness-of-fit" measure via an iterative mathematical programming approach. In this iterative method, sometimes called an "exterior penalty function" approach, the second component is gradually weighted more strongly relative to the first component, so that in later iterations adjustments are made primarily to make the adjusted matrix satisfy the ultrametric inequality. On each iteration, adjustments are made to the entries of D^T in the direction of "steepest descent"; that is, the adjustments are designed to decrease the value of the badness-of-fit measure as rapidly as possible. The algorithm is terminated when the badness-of-fit measure fails to decrease across several iterations. A more formal description of this algorithm is given in Appendix A. The algorithm can be extended easily to handle data matrices with missing entries (De Soete, 1984c).

Unfortunately, at present the above algorithm is not available on any widely distributed software package (see Appendix B for the availability of tree-fitting software). As mentioned previously, however, approximate methods for fitting ultrametric trees to a proximity matrix exist and are widely available because of their inclusion in standard statistical packages. Specifically, using the agglomerative clustering technique of average-link clustering (Sneath & Sokal, 1973) often leads to the least squares optimal tree, or to a tree that is very close to optimal. Average-link clustering is available on virtually every mass-distribution statistical package. For example, the CLUSTER procedures available in SAS, SPSS, and SYSTAT all provide the method of average-link clustering (also known as the "unweighted pair groups method using arithmetic averages," or "UPGMA"; Sneath & Sokal, 1973). An example is presented in Chapter 4 of fitting an ultrametric tree to proximity data using average-link clustering.

Additive Trees

As noted previously, Buneman (1971) showed that the additive inequality (Equation 2.6) was necessary and sufficient for the representation of a matrix of distances by an additive tree (see also Dobson, 1974). Real data, however, usually do not satisfy the additive inequality. The first methods for fitting additive trees to matrices of data that may not satisfy the additive inequality because of error were described by Carroll and Pruzansky (1975), Cunningham (1978), and Sattath and Tversky (1977). The latter two methods are combinatorial algorithms, whereas the Carroll and Pruzansky procedure utilizes a very different approach. The combinatorial algorithms will be discussed first, followed by the Carroll and Pruzansky and related "mathematical programming" methods.

Unfortunately, Cunningham's (1978) procedure requires the inversion of a square matrix of size $N_Q \times N_Q$, where N_Q is the number of distinct quadruples of objects to be scaled. Because $N_Q = (N)(N-1)(N-2)(N-3)/24$, this procedure is impractical for data sets of even moderate size. The Sattath and Tversky (1977) procedure is relatively efficient and effective, and it has been the most widely used method for fitting additive trees. Corter (1982) produced a modified version of the basic Sattath and Tversky algorithm that gives slightly improved fits in about 10% of randomly generated data sets (Corter, 1992, 1996) at only a slight cost in increased processing time. The basic Sattath and Tversky algorithm and the modification introduced by Corter (1982) are described in some detail below.

The basic Sattath and Tversky (henceforth, ST) algorithm works as follows. First, the proximities are transformed into distance-like dissimilarities. That is, if necessary the data are symmetrized by averaging, converted into dissimilarities by subtracting each entry from the largest similarity, and added to the minimal necessary constant so that the dissimilarities satisfy the triangle inequality. At this point, the data are distance-like numbers; that is, they satisfy the axioms of a metric space.

Now the heart of the agglomerative algorithm commences, in which pairs of objects are selected to be clustered together. At each step of the algorithm, one or more pairs (up to $N/2$) of objects may be combined. When a particular pair of objects, x and y, are combined in a given step, the matrix of proximities is then collapsed, with a single new row (and column) of the matrix replacing those for x and y for the next step.

At each step, pairs of objects to be combined are selected in the following way. At the beginning of the step, all possible quadruples of objects (x, y, u, v) are looked at in turn, and for each quadruple the following sums are computed:

$$S1 = d(x, y) + d(u, v)$$

$$S2 = d(x, u) + d(y, v)$$

$$S3 = d(x, v) + d(y, u) \,. \tag{3.2}$$

If the true tree structure of this particular quadruple is such that x and y are nearest neighbors, as are u and v (see Figure 2.3), then the inequality of Equation 2.6 should hold:

$$d(x, y) + d(u, v) < d(x, u) + d(y, v) = d(x, v) + d(y, u)$$

$$S1 < S2 = S3 \,. \tag{3.3}$$

If this inequality is found to hold in this exact form for (x, y, u, v), then this is considered to be evidence that x and y should be neighbors in the tree (i.e., cluster together to form a node), as should u and v. Thus, the pairs (x, y) and (u, v) are given "neighbor scores" of 2 for this quadruple. If instead it is found that $S1 < S2 < S3$ (that is, the two larger sums are not equal), then the neighbor scores of the pairs of objects corresponding to sum $S2$ (i.e., pairs (x, u) and (y, v)) are incremented by 1 as well. This procedure is repeated over all N_Q quadruples of objects, and the neighbor scores for each pair of objects (x, y) are summed across quadruples. The resulting neighbor score for x and y, $N(x, y)$, can be thought of as a robust measure of "tree closeness" for the two objects. If the proximity matrix perfectly reflects a tree structure, then x and y will receive a score of 2 in each of the $(n - 2)(n - 3)/2$ quadruples involving them, and $N(x, y)$ will be equal to $(n - 2)(n - 3)$, its maximal possible value. For data containing errors (that is, that do not correspond perfectly to a tree), the maximal neighbor score in the matrix generally will be less than this value.

Now the neighbor scores for every possible pair of objects are compared. The simplest variant of the ST algorithm would now look for the maximal entry in this neighbor score matrix (which may not be unique) and mark the corresponding pair of objects to be combined in this step. The two objects are joined, the arc lengths corresponding to each object are calculated, the size of the proximity matrix is reduced by 1, and the next step commences.

This simple variant of the algorithm is relatively inefficient because looking through all possible quadruples of objects on the ith step requires processing time approximately proportional to N_i raised to the fourth power, where N_i is the number of objects remaining at the ith step. In addition, in this simple variant of the algorithm there will be $n - 3$ steps in the sequential algorithm. Thus, the processing time required for this algorithm grows rapidly with the number of objects.

Several modifications to this simplest variant of the algorithm can be made, however, in order to improve efficiency. First, rather than combining only that pair of objects corresponding to the largest entry in the neighbor score matrix, in the ST (1977) algorithm all pairs that are *mutual nearest neighbors* are combined at a single step. Object y is defined to be x's nearest neighbor if $N(x, y) = MAX[N(x, z)]$ for all z. Using this more liberal way of identifying pairs of objects to be combined on a single step of the algorithm, up to $N_i/2$ pairs may be combined at step i.

Problems can arise, however, in using this criterion. For example, sometimes the nearest-neighbor relationship is not mutual: x's nearest neighbor is y, but y's nearest neighbor is w. Also, ties sometimes occur, so that both y and w have maximal neighbor scores with x: $N(x, y) = N(x, w) = MAX[N(x, z)]$ for all z. Corter's (1982) modification (algorithm STC) to the basic ST method consists of a relatively sophisticated way of responding to these ambiguous situations. In either of these cases, the problem is to decide if y or w should be clustered with x at this step. This ambiguity is resolved by use of a metric criterion that involves computing all possible pairwise distances among objects x, y, w, and T, where T is a "generalized object" consisting of all objects not in the set (x, y, w). The three sums

$$S1 = d(x, y) + d(w, T)$$

$$S2 = d(x, w) + d(y, T)$$

$$S3 = d(x, T) + d(y, w) \tag{3.4}$$

are then computed, and the "true" tree structure is then inferred by observing which of these sums is minimal. For example, if S1 is minimal, it can be concluded that y rather than w should join x at this step. This method of augmenting the neighbor score information to select pairs of objects to be combined at the current step of the algorithm results in improved performance for the STC algorithm (Corter, 1982) over the original ST algorithm (Sattath & Tversky, 1977). In a simulation study (Corter, 1992, 1996), the STC algorithm gave a slightly improved fit (corresponding in most instances to approximately 1% of proportion of variance accounted for, or PVAF) in about 10% of cases, at only a slight cost in additional computation time.

Recently, other combinatoric algorithms for fitting additive trees have been proposed. For example, Corter (1992, 1996) developed the least squares test used in the STC algorithm for breaking ties in the neighbor-count matrix into a new algorithm for fitting additive trees. The resulting method, termed the "generalized triples" (GT) algorithm, is in principle more efficient than the basic ST and STC algorithms because at each step it looks through only the set of all *triples* of objects rather than all *quadruples* of objects, reducing the search set by a factor of $(N_i - 4)$. Because more calculation is needed for each triple in the GT algorithm compared with the amount needed for each quadruple in the ST and STC algorithms, and because fewer pairs tend to be combined at each step in the GT algorithm, the ST and STC algorithms are less costly computationally for small- and moderate-sized data sets (Corter, 1992, 1996).

Other combinatoric methods for fitting additive trees recently have been described by researchers (e.g., Abdi, Barthélemy, & Luong, 1984; Barthélemy & Guénoche, 1991). In a limited simulation study of five of these algorithms by Barthélemy and Guénoche (1991), results indicated that four of the five algorithms performed worse than simple average-link clustering. The one method that outperformed average-link clustering, the "method of reduction," was the most expensive computationally, requiring more than 30 times the computation time required for any of the other methods. Because of these questions about performance and the lack of widely available software implementing the algorithms, these methods probably will remain mainly of theoretical interest.

The above additive tree-fitting algorithms are examples of "combinatoric" algorithms; that is, they work by examining all possible four-element combinations of objects in order to find some optimal set of objects to be combined at each step. One objection that some researchers have to such algorithms is that proofs that these algorithms find the optimal tree solution can be constructed easily only for the case of errorless data (i.e., that satisfy the additive inequality). Therefore, other researchers have proposed iterative gradient methods that have better-understood optimality properties.

The first such approach was by Carroll and Pruzansky (1975). Their method is based on a result (Carroll, 1976; Sattath & Tversky, 1977) proving that distances in an additive tree D_A can be decomposed into two components, an ultrametric tree component D_U and a component D_S reflecting the distance matrix corresponding to a "singular tree" or "star" graph: $D_A = D_U + D_S$. The algorithm, an alternating least squares method, first fixes estimates of the parameters of the singular tree, then seeks to find the best-fitting ultrametric tree. Next it seeks the best estimates of the singular tree parameters, conditional on that estimated ultrametric tree. These steps are repeated until convergence occurs.

Another least squares method for fitting additive trees was introduced by De Soete (1983). His algorithm operates directly on the matrix of data dissimilarities, adjusting elements of the matrix in the direction of "steepest descent," that is, in the direction that most rapidly decreases the value of a badness-of-fit criterion. As in the Carroll-Pruzansky-De Soete method for fitting ultrametric trees described earlier, this badness-of-fit measure incorporates two components, the first part measuring how poorly the adjusted matrix corresponds to the original data matrix and the second part measuring if and how badly the adjusted matrix violates the additive inequality (Equation 2.6). Again, the algorithm proceeds iteratively, with the second component of the penalty function being weighted more and more heavily in later iterations, in order to ensure that the final adjusted matrix satisfies the additive inequality. The matrix that is finally obtained should satisfy the inequality and should be the closest matrix to the original data that does so. When this final adjusted matrix is obtained, any of several procedures (e.g., the Sattath & Tversky method) can be applied to construct the actual tree corresponding to the final matrix satisfying the additive inequality.

One advantage of such a "mathematical programming" approach is that under certain assumptions about the shape of the function relating the badness-of-fit measure to the parameter space, it can be guaranteed to find the least squares optimal solution. Also, like the Carroll-Pruzansky-De Soete algorithm for fitting ultrametric trees, the method can be generalized to accommodate more complicated problems such as fitting additive trees to incomplete data (De Soete, 1984a) and more complicated models such as those discussed in the next section. Disadvantages of the mathematical programming approaches include higher computational cost compared with the Sattath and Tversky algorithm, the possibility of convergence to a local minimum rather than a global minimum solution (cf. Kruskal & Wish, 1978), and the fact that the end product of the procedure is merely a matrix of distances satisfying the additive inequality, so that the actual construction of the tree graph remains to be performed. Because of these limitations and because the combinatoric Sattath-Tversky-Corter (STC) algorithm (Corter, 1982) is now available in at least one widely available statistics package (see Appendix B), the STC method may be the most practical choice for the researcher interested in applying additive trees.

Multiple Proximity Matrices (3-way 2-mode data)

Sometimes a researcher will be faced with a situation in which there are several proximity matrices to be analyzed. For example, a sample of 10 consumers may each provide a matrix of similarity ratings among 15 products, resulting in ten 15×15 matrices to be analyzed. Such data are referred to as "3-way 2-mode" data (Arabie, Carroll, & DeSarbo, 1987) because there are 3 "ways" or dimensions to the data array (subjects × stimuli × stimuli) and 2 "modes" (distinct sets of objects being analyzed: consumers and products).

One approach to analyzing such data via tree models might be to fit an ultrametric (or additive) tree to each matrix separately. This strategy would be time-consuming and costly, and the structures of the obtained individual trees might be more prone to reflect error than would a group solution. Another simple data-analytic strategy might be to average the 10 matrices into a single matrix of group data and then fit a tree to that single matrix. This strategy, however, might lose important information about individual differences in knowledge or preference. A more elegant approach to analyzing such "3-way 2-mode" data is to fit a model incorporating the assumption that every subject has the same tree structure underlying their judgments but that individual subjects may weight clusters differently. In terms of the obtained solution, this means that every subject will have the same tree, but for subject 1 the branches of the tree may have different weights or lengths than for subject 2. This model, termed the INDTREES model, was introduced by Carroll, Clark, and DeSarbo (1984), who also described a mathematical programming approach to fitting the model.

Proximities Between Two Sets of Objects (2-way 2-mode data)

Sometimes proximity data come in rectangular form. That is, the data consist of a matrix of proximities between two distinct classes of objects: N "row" objects and M "column" objects. For example, ratings by N subjects of how strongly they endorse each of M attitude items may be interpreted as measuring how "close" each subject is to each item. Scaling analyses of such 2-way 2-mode data are often termed *unfolding* analyses, and their goal is to find a "joint space" that represents both row objects (e.g., people) and column objects (e.g., items) in the same space, such that an individual subject is located near those items that he or she tends to endorse more strongly. Spatial unfolding, as performed by such programs as KYST, ALSCAL, or MDPREF, is a more familiar case than unfolding analyses with tree models, although recent work has explored the use of stochastic tree unfolding (STUN) models for probabilistic choice data (Carroll, DeSarbo, & De Soete, 1988, 1989; De Soete & Carroll, 1991).

Two articles have proposed methods for fitting trees to rectangular *proximity* matrices. Furnas (1980) gave necessary and sufficient conditions for the representation of a rectangular proximity matrix by a tree, and De Soete, DeSarbo, Furnas, and Carroll (1984) provided least squares algorithms for fitting either ultrametric or additive trees to such rectangular proximity matrices.

Because most social science researchers will not have access to these specialized algorithms, it seems useful to point out that if the researcher is interested primarily in the proximities among only one set of objects (for example, among the attitude items that were the column objects of the previous example), then an alternative data-analytic strategy is available. This method is first to compute some sort of similarity coefficients (e.g., Euclidean distances or correlations) among the column objects to obtain a 2-way 1-mode proximity matrix (see, e.g., Aldenderfer & Blashfield, 1984), then to use one of the standard tree-fitting algorithms for 2-way 1-mode data (e.g., Corter, 1982; De Soete, 1984a; Sattath & Tversky, 1977). This analysis will provide a tree containing only attitude items, not a "joint space" tree containing both people and items. A second possible motivation for performing this simpler analysis is that unfolding methods tend to suffer from some instability; that is, they tend to find degenerate trees, probably in part because they are fitting a large number of parameters. In fact, the joint tree solution has certain insurmountable nonuniquenesses. That is, the joint tree algorithm, for mathematical reasons, may not be able to distinguish between certain solutions that have different within-set structure (De Soete et al., 1984).

4. PRACTICAL ISSUES AND EXAMPLE APPLICATIONS

Some Practical Issues in Fitting Trees to Data

Weighting of Variables in Multivariate Data

Another issue can arise in fitting trees to rectangular matrices of *multivariate* data (as opposed to data that already may be interpreted as proximities) using the strategy of computing similarity coefficients among the row (or column) objects (representing, for example, people) of the rectangular multivariate data matrix. That issue is how best to weight the different column (row) variables in computing a similarity coefficient. The simple approach of weighting them equally in fact constitutes making implicit and arbitrary decisions as to their relative importance, especially if the variables are measured on different scales or if several variables in the set all represent a single concept. These arbitrary decisions can affect the structure of the obtained tree. One potential solution to this problem is to attempt to weight the variables "equally," by standardizing each variable separately to have a mean of 0 and standard deviation of 1 before computing a similarity coefficient. This practice is controversial because it may obscure meaningful structure (Aldenderfer & Blashfield, 1984; Everitt, 1980).

Another potential solution to the weighting problem, one that tends to emphasize rather than obscure hierarchical structure in the data, is to seek the "optimal" weighting of variables, where "optimal" means the set of weights that maximizes the fit of the tree model to the data. This approach was explored by De Soete, DeSarbo, and Carroll (1985) and De Soete (1986, 1988) for ultrametric and additive trees. Milligan (1989) reported a simulation study of De Soete, DeSarbo, and Carroll's methods that showed they perform well in recovering known optimal variable weightings.

Assessing Fit of the Solution

In viewing trees as models of proximity data, a measure of goodness of fit of the model to the data naturally is required. The criterion of sum of squared errors criterion utilized by many of the algorithms discussed in the previous chapter is not a good choice for a standardized measure because its value depends on such factors as the number of data points and the scale of the proximities. A better choice is R^2, the squared correlation between the data proximities and the interobject (path-length) distances in the tree. This measure is interpretable as the proportion of variance accounted for (PVAF) in the data by the model solution. It has been argued (Carroll, 1995) that nonmetric measures of fit, such as Kruskal's stress (Kruskal & Wish, 1978), may be poor choices for assessing the fit of tree models because of the high proportion of tied distances in an ultrametric tree.

Researchers interested in assessing how well their data are fit by a particular tree solution therefore need ways of calculating R^2. Many of the special-purpose tree-fitting programs (e.g., the ADDTREE/P program; Corter, 1982) automatically calculate the value of this and other fit statistics. Researchers using a standard clustering package to fit an ultrametric tree may need to calculate this fit measure themselves because some packages provide only the topological structure of the resulting tree and do not report fit indices, or they provide indices of fit only when the original data were in the form of a rectangular matrix of multivariate data. Appendix C contains specific instructions for how a researcher can use multiple regression to obtain both least squares estimates of tree parameters (i.e., arc lengths) and an overall index, R^2, of fit of the derived tree to the original proximity data. Essentially, the idea is to represent the length of each arc in the tree by a dummy variable, with the pairs of objects constituting the "observations" or cases of the regression analysis. Then a regression model is fit, predicting each data dissimilarity, $d(x, y)$, as the sum of the arc lengths that enter into the path between x and y. Further details are given in Appendix C.

Applications

Example 1: Ultrametric Tree of Organizational Structure

Trees often are used to depict the formal structure of an organization. Most such "organizational charts" are hierarchically organized and often drawn as rooted trees. Any organization also has informal channels of information flow and influence that generally do not mirror the formal structure. Furthermore, the formal structure of an organization at a given point in time may not be optimal, in part because organizations may react only slowly to changes in their environment, such as changing market forces.

As a demonstration exercise, data were gathered from faculty at Teachers College, Columbia University, concerning a hypothetical reorganization of the departmental structure. Teachers College is a large graduate school affiliated with Columbia University, encompassing programs in education, psychology, and the health professions. At the time of the survey, there were 17 separate departments at the school, organized into five divisions.

Questionnaires were distributed to 122 active full-time faculty at Teachers College. In the question of interest here, respondents were asked to nominate up to 15 other departments that it would make sense "administratively and academically" for their own department to be grouped with into a higher-level administrative unit. Efforts were made to ensure that at least two faculty members responded from each department. There were N = 58 responses to this particular question. Data initially were compiled by summing the responses from individual faculty members by department. The result was a 17×17 matrix, presented in Table 4.1, in which each row represents the summed responses from individuals in that department. The entry in the ith row and jth column of this matrix represents the number of individual faculty members in department i who nominated department j as a candidate for affiliation. Table 4.1 also gives the number of respondents from each department, the division that the department was affiliated with (Divisions I-V), and a key that associates a department number (1-17) with the full name of the department and the label used in the tree graph presented below.

This raw data matrix can be considered to represent the proximity of pairs of departments. It is a row-conditional (Carroll & Arabie, 1980; Young, 1980) matrix because there were different numbers of respondents for each row. Thus a value of "2" in one row might mean that 2 out of 2 respondents from that department nominated the corresponding (column) department, whereas in another row with 5 respondents, the same value of "2" means that only $2/5 = 40\%$ of respondents nominated the corresponding department. Consequently, each row of the matrix was normalized by dividing each entry by the number of respondents for that row. The resulting matrix can be considered an unconditional asymmetric proximity matrix.

In order to submit the data to the hierarchical clustering routine, the data were symmetrized by averaging the two halves of the matrix and converted into dissimilarities by subtracting the similarities from the largest possible value (which would be 1.000 in this case, meaning that all the respondents from the "row" department nominated the "column" department and vice versa). It was this normalized and symmetrized matrix that was submitted to a hierarchical clustering program, as described below.

The hierarchical clustering program used was the routine provided by SPSS. The method requested was the "average linkage between groups" method (also known as the "unweighted pair groups method," Sneath & Sokal, 1973), which is the default in SPSS. Like many of the hierarchical clustering routines available in general-purpose statistical software, the CLUSTER routine of SPSS assumes by default that the data provided to it are multivariate profile data, so special instructions must be included to specify that the data are to be interpreted as a proximity matrix.

The ultrametric tree or "dendrogram" produced by CLUSTER is shown in Figure 4.1. The obtained structure accounts for 98% of the variance in the ratings (see Appendix C) and makes a good deal of conceptual sense. For example, there are three large divisions of the tree, corresponding

TABLE 4.1
Summed Number of Nominations
of Column Departments by Respondents in Row Department

Depart-ment	01	02	03	04	05	06	07	08	09	10	11	12	13	14	15	16	17	n
01	0	0	1	2	1	1	0	0	2	1	1	1	0	2	0	1	0	2
02	0	0	0	0	1	0	0	0	0	0	0	0	0	0	1	0	0	2
03	0	0	0	2	1	1	0	0	0	1	1	0	0	1	0	0	0	2
04	3	0	0	0	1	2	0	1	3	3	0	2	0	1	0	3	0	3
05	0	3	3	2	1	0	0	0	1	1	3	1	0	0	4	2	3	5
06	0	0	1	1	0	0	0	4	0	0	1	0	0	3	0	1	0	4
07	0	0	0	0	0	0	0	0	0	1	0	2	1	0	0	0	1	2
08	0	0	0	1	1	1	0	0	0	0	0	0	0	1	1	0	0	2
09	2	0	1	3	1	0	0	2	1	0	0	0	0	2	0	1	1	6
10	2	1	3	1	1	0	2	1	2	0	2	2	1	1	1	1	1	3
11	0	3	0	1	3	1	0	0	1	2	0	0	1	0	3	0	0	4
12	1	0	0	1	0	0	3	0	1	3	0	0	1	0	0	1	1	3
13	0	2	0	1	0	2	2	1	0	0	2	1	0	0	2	1	1	2
14	0	0	0	1	0	1	1	1	1	0	1	0	1	0	1	0	0	4
15	0	6	0	0	6	0	0	1	0	0	4	0	0	0	0	0	0	7
16	0	0	0	3	3	2	0	0	1	1	0	0	0	0	0	0	2	5
17	0	1	0	0	1	0	1	0	0	0	1	1	0	0	1	2	0	2

Number	Label	Division	Full Name of Department
01	arts_edu	IV	The Arts in Education
02	clin_psy	II	Clinical Psychology
03	comp_edu	IV	Communication, Computing, and Technology in Education
04	curric_t	III	Curriculum and Teaching
05	devel_ed	II	Developmental and Educational Psychology
06	ed_admin	III	Educational Administration
07	hlth_nut	V	Health and Nutrition Education
08	adult_ed	III	Higher and Adult Education
09	lang_lit	IV	Languages, Literature, and Social Studies in Education
10	math_sci	IV	Mathematics and Science Education
11	measrmnt	II	Measurement, Evaluation, and Applied Statistics
12	move_sci	IV	Movement Sciences and Education
13	nurse_ed	V	Nursing Education
14	phil_soc	I	Philosophy and the Social Sciences
15	soc_cnsl	II	Social, Organizational, and Counseling Psychology
16	specl_ed	III	Special Education
17	speech_p	II	Speech and Language Pathology and Audiology

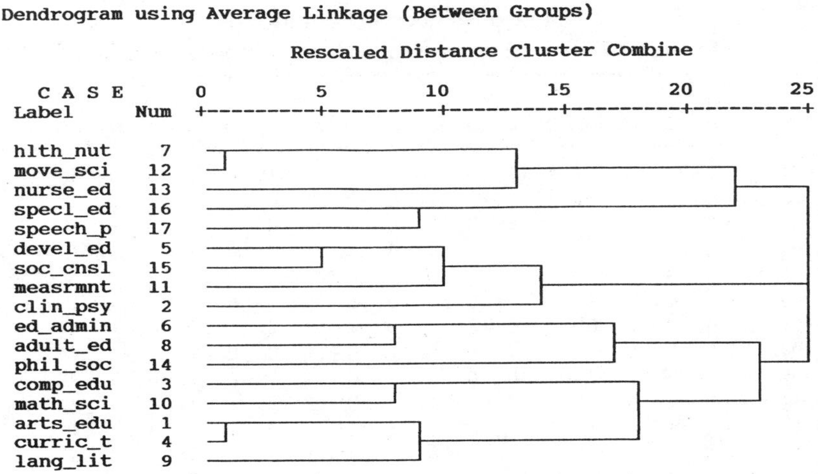

```
Dendrogram using Average Linkage (Between Groups)

                    Rescaled Distance Cluster Combine

  C A S E       0         5        10        15        20        25
  Label    Num  +---------+---------+---------+---------+---------+

  hlth_nut   7
  move_sci  12
  nurse_ed  13
  specl_ed  16
  speech_p  17
  devel_ed   5
  soc_cnsl  15
  measrmnt  11
  clin_psy   2
  ed_admin   6
  adult_ed   8
  phil_soc  14
  comp_edu   3
  math_sci  10
  arts_edu   1
  curric_t   4
  lang_lit   9
```

Figure 4.1. Ultrametric Tree of Departmental Organization Nominations

roughly to the departments concerned with the health-related professions (departments 7, 12, 13, 16, and 17), psychology programs (5, 15, 11, and 2), and more purely educational programs (6, 8, 14, 3, 10, 1, 4, 9). The exception to this neat grouping is the inclusion of department 16 (Special Education) and department 17 (Speech and Language Pathology and Audiology) in the health sciences group. It is easy to see, however, why respondents might group these two departments together: Both are concerned with the problems of individuals with special needs, and these special needs may stem from physiological or health-related causes.

Other subgroupings within this large three-part division also make sense. Within the "purely education" group, departments 3 (Communication, Computing, and Technology in Education) and 10 (Mathematics and Science Education) form a tight cluster. Another cluster consists of the programs mainly concerned with issues of curriculum (departments 1, 4, and 9). The remaining cluster consists of programs concerned more with the organization, administration, and implementation of educational programs (departments 6, 8, and 14).

Note that although the obtained structure makes conceptual sense, it does not reproduce the current organizational chart for the institution. As already pointed out, in the tree solution Special Education (from Division III) and

Speech and Language Pathology and Audiology (from Division II) join with the health sciences (Division V) departments. In addition, Curriculum and Teaching departs from its actual position in Division III to join with the other departments concerned with instruction in specific fields (Division IV). These discrepancies may be taken as indicating that the respondents believe that alternatives exist to the current organizational structure.

The results of this pilot study should be interpreted cautiously. First, only about half of the members of these departments responded to this question, so the results are not guaranteed to be representative of the beliefs of the entire faculty population. Second, the normalization method used—converting raw numbers of nominations into row percentages—may overweight the opinions of individuals from departments with relatively few respondents. Nevertheless, the obtained solution is sensible, and the example illustrates that employees' conceptions of an ideal organizational structure may not always correspond to the formal organizational chart.

Example 2: Additive Tree of Perceived Societal Risks

Johnson and Tversky (1984) collected data concerning how people view various societal risks. The set of risks studied was selected by asking a sample of subjects to list risks that they believed were major causes of death in the United States at that time. A set of 18 risks was selected, including accidental falls, flood, tornados, lightning, electrocution, fire, nuclear accident, toxic chemical spill, homicide, terrorism, war, airplane accidents, traffic accidents, stroke, heart disease, lung cancer, leukemia, and stomach cancer.

Johnson and Tversky asked their subjects to make various types of judgments about these risks. In one task, subjects rated the similarity of each pair of risks on a 1 to 9 scale, where 1 = *very dissimilar* and 9 = *very similar.* In another task, subjects were asked to make a conditional prediction judgment. In the latter task, they were first asked to give an estimate of how many people in the United States die each year from each specific risk. Then a "target" risk (e.g., leukemia) was selected, and the subject was told to suppose that he or she had just learned that many more people die from leukemia than they had estimated. They were then asked to indicate which of the other risks they would like to revise their estimates for, based on this new information. This question was repeated using each risk in turn as a "target." The resulting "conditional prediction" data may also be considered a type of proximity data, because a subject presumably would want to revise his or her estimate for a risk only if that risk is closely related to the target risk for which new information has become available.

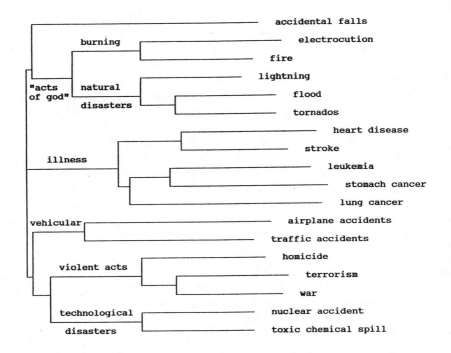

Figure 4.2. Additive Tree of Perceived Similarity of Risks (Johnson & Tversky, 1984)

Johnson and Tversky present an additive tree solution for the prediction data, noting that the obtained tree accounts for a large proportion of the variance in the data ($R^2 = .89$). Figure 4.2 presents an additive tree obtained by analyzing the data from their similarity task with the ADDTREE/P program (Corter, 1982). This tree accounts for 75% of the variance in the similarity rating data ($R^2 = .75$), and the structure is highly interpretable, as shown by the labels added next to certain arcs in the tree. One cluster groups risks sometimes termed "acts of god": tornados, flood, lightning, fire, and electrocution. This cluster is further subdivided into "natural disasters" and "burning." *Accidental falls* is grouped only loosely with these risks, perhaps because although a fall sometimes may be seemingly random or unexplained, in other cases it may be blamed on personal factors such as negligence. The next large cluster groups all the illnesses, subdivided into cancers and coronary problems. Finally, three clusters are all loosely amalgamated into a high-level grouping of all risks that might be caused by another person's negligence or malevolence. These include vehicular accidents, violent acts, and technological disasters.

Thus the tree seems quite interpretable. It is interesting to note that differences exist between the additive tree solution for the similarity ratings (Figure 4.2) and the tree for the prediction data, reported by Johnson and Tversky. For example, in Figure 4.2 *electrocution* and *fire* form a cluster, perhaps because the subjective experience of suffering each type of risk would be similar, or perhaps because these are common household hazards. In the tree based on the prediction data, however, *electrocution* joined with *lightning,* perhaps because a fatality caused by lightning might be described more generally as a case of electrocution. Other minor differences between the trees are discernible, and all seem explainable. Of particular note is the fact that the tree for the prediction data accounts for a much higher proportion of the variance ($R^2 = .89$ versus $R^2 = .75$). This probably is due to the more specific nature of the conditional prediction task. In the similarity rating task, subjects are more free to interpret "similarity" as they please, perhaps leading to different interpretations, and hence different structures, for different individual subjects. These different structures might not all be representable by the same single tree structure, leading to the lower fit.

5. SOME EXTENSIONS OF TREE MODELS

Some interesting special cases and extensions of tree models have been proposed for particular applications. For example, Carroll (1976) discusses tree models in which the conceptual objects being modeled are represented not by leaf nodes alone, as in most of the applications in this book, but by both leaf nodes and internal nodes of the tree (see, e.g., the minimal spanning tree of Figure 1.1). This approach allows the objects themselves to exhibit a hierarchical structure, with some objects being modeled as the "parents" of some other objects.

As an illustration, consider a set of data collected by Miller (1969). These data were collected by asking subjects to sort cards containing the names of body parts (e.g., "head," "arm," "toe," and so forth) into clusters of related objects. Carroll (1976) presents a solution for these data that indeed exhibits a hierarchical object structure, with (for example) leaf nodes for "hand," "palm," and "elbow" joining to a higher node corresponding to the stimulus "arm," which then joins to the top node in the tree, "body."

The combinatoric procedure used to fit this type of tree structure (Carroll & Chang, 1973) was rather inefficient. Furthermore, a moment's reflection should provide another reason why such an algorithm really is not needed: If data indeed satisfy this type of object hierarchy structure, then an additive tree fit to the data should recover the hierarchy by assigning the leaf arc for any "higher" node (e.g., "body") a very small or even zero length (Carroll, 1976).

Another type of special case of tree models consists of applications in which the solution must be constrained in some way. For example, Roskam (1973) discusses the possibility of constraining the weights or lengths of branches in the tree (under this view, an ultrametric tree may be viewed as a constrained case of an additive tree). A more interesting type of constraint, however, is one requiring that the tree have a certain *topology*; for example, requiring that objects A, B, and E together form a cluster (branch) in the tree structure. Finding the best-fitting tree while respecting a constraint of this type is a problem investigated by De Soete, Carroll, and DeSarbo (1987). This type of problem may arise when a theory (or some pragmatic concern) provides a partial structure for the tree but other details of the structure are left unspecified, to be discovered by the algorithm.

The status of trees as special cases of graph models leads to another obvious generalization of tree models, namely allowing arcs of the tree to have directionality. Cunningham (1978) discusses what he terms a *bidirectional tree,* which has two continuous parameters for each arc. For example, the arc from node a to node b will have two weights, one measuring the "length" of the arc in the direction $a \rightarrow b$ and the other measuring the length in the opposite direction. This generalization allows the tree to represent a matrix of asymmetric proximity data, in which the entries above and below the diagonal differ. Because of the greater number of parameters for this bidirectional tree, estimation of the arc lengths is subject to certain indeterminacies (Cunningham, 1978).

Two final extensions of tree models, while quite different in character, are motivated by identical goals. Specifically, the goals are to utilize some of the desirable properties of trees (e.g., the graphical representation of distances by path lengths and importance of clusters by arc lengths) in modeling proximity data that do not have a hierarchical structure (that is, data that fail for substantive reasons to satisfy the ultrametric or additive inequalities). One way of using trees to model such data is to fit *multiple trees* to the proximities (Carroll, 1976; Carroll & Pruzansky, 1975). In the multiple tree model, the dissimilarity between two objects a and b is represented by the *sum* of the distances in two or more trees. Carroll and Corter (1995) report an application of this type of model to some sorting data gathered by Rosenberg and Kim (1975) representing subjects' appraisal of the relatedness of 15 kinship terms in English (e.g., "father," "mother," "cousin," etc.). The two-tree solution obtained by Carroll and Corter included one tree that separated the terms into a female group, a male group, and "cousin" (the only gender-neutral term), plus a second tree with clusters based on generation and collaterality (e.g., "mother" and "father" form one cluster).

A second approach that aims to exploit the readability of tree graphs to represent more general data structures is that of Corter and Tversky (1986), who proposed what they termed the "extended tree." This model extends the notion of a rooted additive tree by introducing marked or labeled segments into the tree structure to represent attributes that "cut across" the tree structure. For example, Corter and Tversky (1986) give an example of an extended tree representing the conceptual similarity of instances of the concept "sports" (obtained by analysis of some data from Smith, Rips, Schoben, Rosch, & Mervis, 1975). The basic tree contains a cluster corresponding to "swimming," "skin diving," and "surfing" (water sports), and another corresponding to "canoeing," "hiking," "camping," and "horseback riding" (wilderness activities). The extended tree adds a marked segment that links "canoeing" to the water sports cluster, because "canoeing" also is a water sport. Thus the device of marked segments can be used to represent these more general (nonhierarchical) patterns of features or attributes, while preserving some of the attractive characteristics of trees.

6. DISCUSSION AND CONCLUSIONS

Using Trees to Find Partitions

In certain applications, researchers are interested only in finding a *partition* of the objects they are studying, that is, a classification into mutually exclusive and exhaustive subsets. For example, a segmentation analysis in market research may seek a classification of consumers into a manageable number of groups that are alike in some fundamental ways, such as buying behavior or attitudes. As another example, a clinical psychologist may be interested in studying a certain clinical population, such as those suffering from posttraumatic stress disorder, in order to discover if there are a number of distinct subtypes within this population. Current standard practice in such applications is for the researcher to use a partitioning algorithm, such as k-means clustering. These programs require that the researcher specify the desired number of clusters. Therefore, if the researcher has no prior beliefs as to the expected number of clusters, it would seem necessary to try a number of solutions, systematically varying the requested number of clusters.

Tree-fitting methods can serve as quick methods for finding useful partitions in applications such as these, particularly in cases in which the researcher has no prior beliefs about the true number of clusters. Thus, an alternative data analysis strategy is to calculate proximities and proceed with a tree-fitting analysis, then examine the tree for a seemingly optimal partition solution. Any "slice" through a rooted tree that severs all the leaf nodes from the root determines a partition. By varying the height at which this slice is made, the researcher easily can assess the quality of different possible partitions into more or fewer clusters.

An example of this use of a tree-fitting technique is described in Corter (1989). He applied the ADDTREE/P program to fit an additive tree to a matrix of similarities among 30 dialects of the Salish language originally spoken by Native Americans from the Pacific Northwest. These similarities were percentages of shared cognates between each pair of dialects, as calculated by Swadesh (1950). The resulting additive tree is shown in Figure 6.1.

The two heavy vertical lines labeled "Swadesh" and "Dyen" represent two proposed classifications (partitions) of these dialects, one by Swadesh himself and the other a later refinement by Dyen (1962). Other partitions are possible; however, the partitions proposed by Swadesh and Dyen can be seen to be particularly good ones, because they "cut" the tree across relatively long internal arcs, each such arc corresponding to a relatively distinct cluster.

It should be noted, however, that the use of tree-fitting methods to substitute for partitioning methods may not always be possible. In particular, with very large data sets, computing and storing the $N(N - 1)/2$ proximities necessary to apply the tree-fitting methods may be impossible or impractical. Because partitioning methods typically operate directly on the rectangular matrix of multivariate data, they may be the only practical choice in such cases.

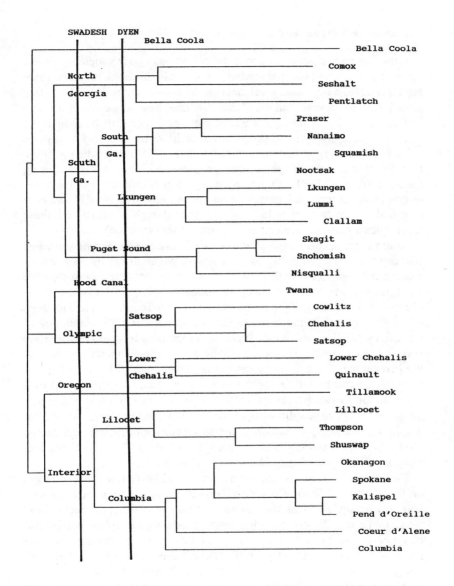

Figure 6.1. Additive Tree and Two Alternative Partitions of 30 Salish Dialects (adapted from Corter, 1989)

Ultrametric Versus Additive Trees

Little has been said so far about the conditions under which one or the other of the two types of tree models discussed in this book might be more appropriate for analyzing a given data set. Mathematically, the additive tree model is more general than the ultrametric tree; thus, any data set that can be fit perfectly by an ultrametric tree also can be fit perfectly by an additive tree. This does not mean in practice that additive trees should always be used. For one thing, it is computationally more difficult to fit an additive tree. By contrast, the weighted average or related hierarchical clustering methods often used to fit ultrametric trees are very efficient, both in terms of computation time and storage requirements, and thus may be the only practical way to fit trees to larger data sets (although, as discussed, these techniques are not guaranteed to find the optimal solution).

Assuming that either type of tree can be fit to a particular data set, when will one model be preferable over the other? We might try to answer such a question based on either theoretical or statistical grounds. If we can make an argument, based on knowledge about the application domain, that the ultrametric inequality is a reasonable constraint to require of the data, then we might prefer the simpler ultrametric tree model from the standpoint of parsimony. To illustrate this, consider the problem of trying to establish the correct "phylogenetic" sequence among a set of languages from data on the percentage of shared cognates between each pair of present-day languages. Assume that differences among the languages are produced by a combination of two processes: random innovations in each separate language and successive splitting up of communities of speakers, so that after a split innovations in the two separate languages occur independently. Under these two assumptions, the present-day dissimilarities among languages will be approximated by the distances in a tree.

The choice between the ultrametric and the additive tree models hinges on the validity of another assumption: If the rates of innovations in each language group are equal, then an ultrametric tree will be appropriate, and we should prefer the simpler (ultrametric) model on grounds of parsimony. If, however, the rates of linguistic innovation in the language groups are believed to differ, then the leaves of the tree will not be equally distant from the root; hence, the additive tree model will be more appropriate.

Alternatively, deciding between the two models might be accomplished by comparing them statistically, that is, by comparing the goodness-of-fit (R^2) measures when the two structures are applied to the same data. Because an additive tree has ($N - 1$) additional parameters (corresponding to the leaf arcs) compared with an ultrametric tree with the same topological structure, it will necessarily fit as well or better. The question nevertheless can be asked: Is the increase in R^2 large enough to justify the use of the additional parameters? Thus, a statistical approach to the question of deciding on the more appropriate tree model would entail calculating R^2 measures (see Appendix C) for both an ultrametric tree and the corresponding additive tree (that is, the additive tree with the same topology). Then the two R^2 values can be compared to determine if the increase in R^2 is significant given the additional number of parameters that were estimated for the additive tree. The standard partial F test used to compare nested regression models can be used for this purpose, even though the usual assumptions concerning independence of errors are not met (Freedman & Lane, 1983).

Trees Versus Spatial Models

Trees and dimensional spaces seem to be very different types of models. Trees portray proximities as being composed of patterns of shared or unique discrete features or properties. Spaces portray proximities as being determined by the differing values of objects on one or more continuous dimensions. An additive tree, however, can represent structures as "spacelike" as a line, and stimulus points in a spatial solution can exhibit clustering into discrete groups.

Are the models, applied to a data set, simply different pictures or interpretations of the same structure? Or do they capture fundamentally different aspects of complex structures, because of some basic mathematical incompatibilities between tree and spatial models? Holman (1972) provided results seeming to show that the latter view is true, that there is a fundamental incompatibility between ultrametric structures and geometric structures such that a given set of proximities are monotonically related either to a low-dimensional spatial representation *or* to an ultrametric tree, but (necessarily) not to both. Critchley and Heiser (1988), however, point out that Holman's conclusions depend on a very strict definition of monotonicity and that ultrametric trees can be represented perfectly in one dimension if tied dissimilarities in the tree are allowed to become untied in the spatial representation.

This view, that the models are not completely incompatible, seems supported by the experiences of researchers who have applied both types of models to the same data set. For example, it is often possible to plot a tree representation of a proximity matrix as a compact series of nested contours in a 2-dimensional MDS solution for the same data (e.g., Figure 7 of Carroll, 1976; Figure 6 of Shepard, 1980), indicating that objects grouped as "near" in the tree are also plotted close together in the MDS solution. Other cases can be found, however, in which the tree and spatial solutions seem incompatible. For example, Sattath and Tversky (1977) point out that the simple case of an evenly spaced grid of points on a plane cannot be represented as a tree, whereas a singular tree (in which there is only a single internal node) cannot be represented in a low-dimensional space.

For more complex structures, a tree and a space may represent different real aspects of the proximity relations among objects. One possible approach to reconciling differences between the tree and spatial representations would be to fit a "hybrid" model that combines elements of both spatial and cluster models (Carroll, 1976; Degerman, 1970). Some researchers have explored methods for fitting hybrid models (Carroll & Pruzansky, 1975, 1980; Winsberg & Carroll, 1989). At present, however, these methods are not widely available.

Consequently, the researcher interested in applying tree and/or MDS models to a specific set of proximity data will often face the situation of trying to decide whether a tree or spatial model is more appropriate. This problem can be approached in several ways. One criterion that could be used to decide whether a tree or a spatial solution is preferable is *interpretability* of the solution. The more interpretable solution may be more useful simply because it can be explained more readily or because it generates more insights into the nature of the relations among the scaled objects.

Another approach commonly used to decide between models is to compare them as to how well they *fit* the data. This approach is difficult to apply in choosing between spatial and tree representations for several reasons. First, MDS programs sometimes report only a monotonic measure of fit (e.g., stress), whereas tree-fitting programs usually report R^2 (the proportion of variance in the data accounted for by the tree), or sometimes no fit measure at all. To directly compare fit for a tree and a space, the same fit statistic should be used for both solutions. R^2 is perhaps the best choice, because even nonmetric MDS algorithms usually do a good job of recovering the metric structure in proximity data (Young, 1970). Depending on the MDS program used, the researcher may have to calculate this R^2 value for the spatial solution by computing model distances from the coordinates of the points on the dimensions.

The second problem in comparing fit between a space and a tree arises because fit of a spatial solution almost always can be improved by increasing the dimensionality of the solution. In fact, any set of distances among N points always can be fit perfectly by a space of $N - 1$ dimensions. Consequently, finding that a 5-dimensional space has a higher R^2 than does an additive tree solution for the same data does not necessarily mean that the data is more "spacelike" than "treelike."

In contrast, trees have a fixed number of real-valued parameters (although some of these parameters may be equal to 0). Ultrametric trees require the estimation of $N - 1$ real-valued parameters, associated with the heights of nodes. Thus an ultrametric tree seems comparable in terms of number of parameters to a 1-dimensional space, which has $N - 1$ real parameters, namely the coordinates of the points on the dimension (minus 1 arbitrary scale factor). An additive tree has $2N - 3$ real parameters, corresponding to the length associated with each arc in the tree. This is roughly comparable to the number of parameters for a 2-dimensional spatial configuration. It should be noted, however, that the structure of the tree itself may be thought of as a set of parameters, and it is not at all clear how, or even whether, to count them. This issue creates more confusion in trying to compare the fit of trees and spaces.

Note that these two criteria of interpretability and fit cannot be used in a *predictive* way to select between a tree and a spatial solution. In order to apply the criteria to judge which solution seems better, both the tree and MDS analyses must be performed. It seems obvious to ask whether there are ways to predict whether a spatial or tree model will be preferable for a given set of proximity data. According to scaling lore, the answer to this question is "yes." In general, objects differing on continuous attributes (e.g., income, age, height, weight, or location) might be modeled better as points in a space, whereas objects differing on categorical attributes (e.g., gender, nationality, or political party) might exhibit a clustering or treelike structure. In specific fields of application, these very general heuristic rules may be augmented by more specific ones. For example, in applications to psychological similarity (in which the data are similarities or confusabilities among stimuli), the usual distinction is between perceptual and conceptual stimuli. If the objects to be scaled are perceptual stimuli (e.g., colors or tones) and/or are expected to vary along some set of continuous dimensions, then a spatial model might be more appropriate. If, on the other hand, the stimuli are more conceptual in nature (e.g., category names, product descriptions, etc.) and/or seem to vary according to whether each stimulus possesses various discrete properties, a tree model might be preferable. When the objects are chosen, identified, or distinguished by some sort of sequential process, tree structures are especially likely to result (e.g., Tverksy & Sattath, 1979).

In fields other than psychology, different particular types of phenomena may be suspected of producing tree structures. For example, in sociological and historical fields, any set of objects that has arisen through an evolutionary process of "splitting" or successive differentiation (e.g., the evolution of species or languages) is likely to be modeled successfully by some sort of tree model. When spatial or geographic influences help to determine the proximity relations (e.g., in modeling trading or communication patterns), a spatial model might be more appropriate.

Some researchers have attempted to find diagnostic statistics (besides fit measures) that might be useful in distinguishing proximity data that are better modeled by spaces from data that are better modeled by trees. Sattath and Tversky (1977) listed some characteristic properties of the distribution of a set of dissimilarities that can be modeled as a tree. Pruzansky, Tversky, and Carroll (1982) investigated the distribution of two diagnostic statistics, *skewness* and *elongation of triples*, for additive trees and 2-dimensional spaces. They concluded that trees tend to produce distributions of dissimilarities that are negatively skewed (i.e., that have few small distances and many large ones) and have a relatively high proportion of elongated triples. Tversky and Hutchinson (1986) investigated two other potential diagnostic statistics, centrality and reciprocity. *Centrality* is an index that measures to what extent one or several stimuli are "central," that is, the nearest neighbors of many other points in the space. *Reciprocity* measures to what extent the nearest neighbor relationship is reciprocal, that is, if object i is j's nearest neighbor, then j is i's nearest neighbor. Tversky and Hutchinson (1986) found that high values of either centrality or reciprocity may be used to rule out low-dimensional ($R = 2$ or 3) spatial models but were compatible with trees.

Conclusions

Ultrametric and additive trees offer convenient and powerful graphical displays of the similarities or distances among objects. In particular, trees provide a means of representing *hierarchical structure* in proximity data. Trees and related cluster models provide a useful alternative to the more widely used spatial models of proximity such as principal components analysis (PCA) or multidimensional scaling (MDS). Trees have natural interpretations in terms of sets of objects and features possessed by objects.

As a result of recent developments in algorithms and software, tree models are now available for use by the nonspecialist and applicable to many types of data. Algorithms for fitting trees are simpler and faster than those for fitting more complicated cluster models, which means that trees are often the only type of discrete-feature or nonspatial model to be practical in fitting a proximity matrix. In summary, trees are useful to the social science researcher both as graphical data analysis tools and as models of similarity relations.

APPENDIX A: MATHEMATICAL PROGRAMMING

In order to illustrate the principles involved in "mathematical programming" approaches to fitting trees to proximity data, the Carroll-Pruzansky-De Soete algorithm (Carroll & Pruzansky, 1975; De Soete, 1984b, 1984c) for fitting ultrametric trees is described here somewhat more formally. The term *mathematical programming* comes from the field of operations research and refers to a class of methods for optimizing objective functions under constraints.

The problem of finding the best-fitting ultrametric tree for a set of proximity data can be viewed as a *constrained optimization problem*. The goal is to minimize a loss function measuring the badness of fit of a matrix of model (tree) distances, $\hat{D}$, to a matrix of data dissimilarities, D, subject to the constraint that the model distances satisfy the ultrametric inequality. That is,

$$\text{Minimize } L(\hat{D}) = \Sigma(d_{ij} - \hat{d}_{ij})^2$$

$$\text{subject to } \hat{d}_{ij} \leq \text{MAX}[\hat{d}_{ik}, \hat{d}_{jk}] \text{ for all } i, j, k \qquad (A.1)$$

where the summation in the loss function L is over all pairs (i, j). This constrained optimization problem can be solved by a "sequential unconstrained minimization technique" (De Soete, 1984c), in which the following augmented function is sequentially minimized for an increasing sequence of ρ:

$$\Phi(\hat{D}, \rho) = L(\hat{D}) + \rho P(\hat{D}) \ (\rho > 0). \qquad (A.2)$$

$P(\hat{D})$ is a weighted penalty function that measures the extent to which matrix $\hat{D}$ violates the ultrametric inequality:

$$P(\hat{D}) = \Sigma(\hat{d}_{ik} - \hat{d}_{jk})^2, \qquad (A.3)$$

where the summation is only over the set of ordered triples of objects (i, j, k) for which $\hat{d}_{ij} \leq \text{MIN}[\hat{d}_{ik}, \hat{d}_{jk}]$ and $\hat{d}_{ik} \neq \hat{d}_{jk}$, that is, the set of triples for which the ultrametric inequality is violated.

In De Soete's (1984b, 1984c) version of the method, $\hat{D}$, the matrix of model dissimilarities, is initialized to some value $\hat{D}_0$ (one possibility is to set this equal to D plus a small amount of random error). The constant ρ is initialized to equal $L(\hat{D}_0)/P(\hat{D}_0)$. Then on step t of the algorithm, $\hat{D}_{t-1}$ is transformed to that value $\hat{D}_t$ that minimizes $\Phi(\hat{D}, \rho_t)$. This step is an unconstrained optimization problem for which the (iterative) conjugate gradient method (Powell, 1977) is used. This step is repeated, increasing the value of ρ on each successive step (e.g., $\rho_{t+1} = 10\rho_t$) until matrix $\hat{D}$ converges to some value. The resulting matrix should be the optimal tree solution; that is, it should satisfy the ultrametric inequality and be the closest matrix to D that does so. The actual tree corresponding to $\hat{D}$ then can be constructed by running some simple agglomerative clustering procedure on matrix $\hat{D}$. For example, because the distances in $\hat{D}$ satisfy the ultrametric inequality, either single-link, complete-link, or average-link clustering, as implemented in various statistical packages, could be used to recover the correct tree structure.

APPENDIX B: AVAILABILITY OF SOFTWARE FOR FITTING TREES

The algorithms described in this book vary widely in their availability. Some, such as the sequential agglomerative method for fitting ultrametric trees known as "average-link clustering" (also known as the "unweighted pair groups method using arithmetic averages," or "UPGMA"; Sneath & Sokal, 1973), are available in several widely distributed statistical packages. For example, the CLUSTER procedures of SAS, SPSS, and SYSTAT all include this method.

The only algorithm for fitting additive trees that is currently available in a widely used statistical package is the Sattath-Tversky-Corter (STC) algorithm (Corter, 1982). This method is available in the latest release (version 6.0) of SYSTAT for DOS, available from SPSS Inc., 444 N. Michigan Avenue, Chicago, IL 60611, (312) 329-3500.

A stand-alone DOS-executable version of the ADDTREE/P program (Corter, 1982) written in the PASCAL language is also available free of charge from the author. Those with access to a file transfer program such as FTP on the Internet can access and retrieve the DOS-executable version as follows. First, FTP to ftp.ilt.columbia.edu and login as "anonymous," then connect ("cd") to the directory "users/corter." The program and documentation files then can be retrieved with the usual GET command. Gopher users can access the files by gophering to gopher.ilt.columbia.edu and connecting to "users/corter." Finally, PASCAL source code for the ADDTREE/P program is maintained at an Internet site, the "netlib/mds" library at AT&T Bell Labs. This resource can be accessed via e-mail, by sending a message to the Internet address netlib@research.att.com containing only the message

    send readme index from mds

as a single line.

The return message will contain general information about netlib ("readme") and a list of the programs available ("index"). You may request items by sending additional mail messages to netlib. For example, to request the ADDTREE/P source code, send the following message to netlib@research.att.com

    send addtree.pas from mds

To get documentation, send the message

    send addtree_manual from mds

Software implementing other algorithms described in this book may in some cases be available from the authors of the original articles describing the methods. Often programs are distributed in the form of source code (usually FORTRAN) that must be compiled on the requester's computer.

APPENDIX C: ESTIMATING FIT OF
A TREE USING MULTIPLE REGRESSION

This section describes how the fit (R^2) of a tree structure to a proximity matrix, as well as estimates of the appropriate arc lengths for calculating path-length distances, can be obtained using a multiple regression package. In this method, it is assumed that only the structure of the tree is known, that is, the order in which objects and clusters combine, moving from the leaves to the root of the tree. The lengths of arcs in the tree are the parameters (regression coefficients) to be estimated. The fit of the regression model, as measured by R^2, indicates the fit of the tree model to the proximity data. This regression method of estimation is useful because sometimes a tree structure is suggested by theory, not derived using a software package. In addition, some software does not provide this particular index of linear fit. The regression method is illustrated using two examples from the text, specifically, the additive tree of Figure 2.2 and the ultrametric tree of Figure 2.1.

To see how to set up the estimation problem for the additive tree of Figure 2.2 as a multiple regression, we begin by writing the data dissimilarities as a vector. In this analysis, the data dissimilarities will be the dependent or criterion variable (usually called variable y in a regression, but here referred to as variable d). For this problem the dissimilarities to be predicted are:

$$d = \begin{array}{r} 15 \\ 20 \\ 25 \\ 18 \\ 23 \\ 6 \\ 20 \\ 25 \\ 20 \\ 18 \end{array} \qquad (C.1)$$

Next, a model matrix ($\mathbf{X}$) is defined that specifies which parameters (arc lengths) enter into which interobject distances in the additive tree. The $\mathbf{X}$ matrix contains $N(N-1)/2$ rows (equal to the number of proximity values). In this $\mathbf{X}$ matrix, each entry is set equal to 1 if the parameter (arc length) corresponding to that column is included in the path between the pair of objects corresponding to that row. The final important component of the regression model is a vector b of $2N - 3$ parameters, the unknown quantities to be estimated. In regression terminology, these unknowns are the regression coefficients. In terms of the tree, they are the arc length estimates. With these components defined, the multiple regression model for the example of Figure 2.2 can be written in matrix notation as:

$$d = \mathbf{X}b + e$$

(B, A)	15		1	1	0	0	0	0	0	b_1		e_1
(C, A)	20		1	0	1	0	0	1	1	b_2		e_2
(C, B)	25		0	1	1	0	0	1	1	b_3		e_3
(D, A)	18		1	0	0	1	0	1	1	b_4		e_4
(D, B)	23	=	0	1	0	1	0	1	1	b_5	+	e_5
(D, C)	6		0	0	1	1	0	0	0	b_6		e_6
(E, A)	20		1	0	0	0	1	1	0	b_7		e_7
(E, B)	25		0	1	0	0	1	1	0			e_8
(E, C)	20		0	0	1	0	1	0	1			e_9
(E, D)	18		0	0	0	1	1	0	1			e_{10} (C.2)

In this example, the parameters b_1 through b_7 represent the arc lengths, with b_1–b_5 representing the leaf arcs corresponding to objects A through E, b_6 representing the arc joining cluster (A, B) to the root, and b_7 representing the arc joining cluster (C, D) to the root. We can see from this matrix formulation that, for example, the (model) path length between objects B and A is given by $\hat{d}(A, B) = b_1 + b_2$.

This matrix formulation of the multiple regression problem can be translated easily into a computer data file suitable for analysis by standard software for multiple regression. One column of numbers in the data file will be d, the vector of dissimilarities (the dependent variable of the regression). The other $2N - 3$ columns will be the columns of the $\mathbf{X}$ matrix, representing the path-length distances into which the corresponding arc enters. Thus the following data file would be appropriate:

```
15  1  1  0  0  0  0  0
20  1  0  1  0  0  1  1
25  0  1  1  0  0  1  1
18  1  0  0  1  0  1  1
23  0  1  0  1  0  1  1
 6  0  0  1  1  0  0  0
```

58

20	1	0	0	0	1	1	0
25	0	1	0	0	1	1	0
20	0	0	1	0	1	0	1
18	0	0	0	1	1	0	1

(C.3)

Note that it is necessary to request the regression model to be fit without a constant (intercept) term. Otherwise, the set of predictors will not be independent, and error messages and unpredictable behavior may result.

When the above regression problem is analyzed using a standard regression package, the following estimates of parameters are obtained: $b_1 = 5.0$, $b_2 = 10.0$, $b_3 = 4.0$, $b_4 = 2.0$, $b_5 = 10.0$, $b_6 = 5.0$, and $b_7 = 6.0$. These results correspond perfectly with the arc lengths given in Figure 2.2. Furthermore, the fit of the model is perfect ($R^2 = 1.00$), as expected for these artificial data that were made up so as to perfectly satisfy the additive inequality.

The fit (R^2) and parameter estimates of an ultrametric tree can be estimated by a similar procedure. The lengths of certain arcs in an ultrametric tree, however, are constrained by values of other arcs; this means that the number of variables used in the multiple regression will be fewer than the apparent number of arcs. Specifically, there are apparently $2N - 3$ arcs (just as for an additive tree), but only $N - 1$ of them correspond to independent parameters to be estimated.

Estimation of the ultrametric tree path-length parameters begins, as it does in the case of an additive tree, by writing the dissimilarities as a vector. Then the **X** (model) matrix is defined. To do this, we must specify the way in which particular arcs enter into the path-length distances between objects. For example, in the ultrametric tree of Figure 2.1, the first cluster formed (moving from the leaves to the root) consists of *shoplifting* (*sh*) and *burglary* (*bu*). The length of the arc connecting the leaf for *shoplifting* (*sh*) to this node where *sh* and *bu* combine is one of the parameters to be estimated (we also can call this value the "height" of the node). Note that once we specify the length of this arc, we also know the length of the arc connecting *burglary* (*bu*) to the same node, because in an ultrametric tree the leaves of the tree are constrained to be equally distant from the root (and equally distant from any common ancestor node). The path length between *sh* and *bu* therefore is equal to twice this arc length. For this reason, we enter a "2" in the appropriate row and column of the **X** matrix to define the distance as being twice the arc length.

Now we can proceed to set up the rest of the regression equation. As already noted, the vector of data dissimilarities constitutes the dependent or criterion variable *d* of the analysis, and the estimated path-length distances in the tree will correspond to the estimated values $\hat{d}$. In the matrix formulation of the regression equation, the presence or absence of arc lengths in a particular path (say, between objects u and v) defines the predictor variables (the columns of matrix $\mathbf{X}$), and the arc lengths are represented by the unknown regression coefficients to be estimated (vector b). The problem then can be written:

$$d = \mathbf{X}b + e$$

(bu, ar)	8		0	0	2	0		b_1		e_1
(pe, ar)	10		0	0	0	2		b_2		e_2
(pe, bu)	10		0	0	0	2		b_3		e_3
(sh, ar)	8		0	0	2	0		b_4		e_4
(sh, bu)	2	=	2	0	0	0			+	e_5
(sh, pe)	10		0	0	0	2				e_6
(va, ar)	4		0	2	0	0				e_7
(va, bu)	8		0	0	2	0				e_8
(va, pe)	10		0	0	0	2				e_9
(va, sh)	8		0	0	2	0				e_{10}

(C.4)

Note that there are five objects but only $N - 1 = 4$ parameters to be estimated. Each parameter corresponds to an element of vector b and to a column of matrix $\mathbf{X}$. The first parameter, b_1, can be thought of as representing the height of the node corresponding to the cluster consisting of *shoplifting* (sh) and *burglary* (bu). The path length between sh and bu is equal to twice the height of this node, hence the entry in the $\mathbf{X}$ matrix in the row corresponding to (sh, bu) and the column corresponding to b_1 is the value 2, because $\hat{d}(sh, bu) = 2b_1$. Parameter b_2 has a similar interpretation: Its estimate gives the height of the node joining *vandalism* (va) and *arson* (ar).

Parameter b_3 has a slightly more complex interpretation: It represents the height of the node where the cluster (sh, bu) joins with cluster (va, ar). Thus the estimated (tree) distance between any object in the first cluster (e.g., *shoplifting*) and any object in the second cluster (e.g., *vandalism*) is given by $\hat{d}(sh, va) = 2b_3$. Parameter b_3 thus does not correspond directly to any arc length; the length of the arcs joining cluster (sh, bu) with cluster (sh, bu, va, ar) must be obtained by subtracting the two node heights, $b_3 - b_1$.

Finally, the last parameter in the tree is b_4, representing the height at which *perjury* joins the other four objects (the root of the tree). Looking at the $\mathbf{X}$ matrix, we can see that parameter b_4 enters into each distance

60

involving perjury and one of the remaining four crimes (e.g., $\hat{d}(pe, ar)$ = 2b$_4$). The length of the arc joining the leaf for *perjury* to the root is given by the estimated value of this parameter; the length of the arc connecting node (*sh, bu, va, ar*) to the root must be obtained by subtraction, $b_4 - b_3$.

The data for the regression analysis can be entered into a computer file in essentially the format given above. The first column of numbers entered will correspond to the vector of data dissimilarities, and the next four columns will correspond to the columns of the **X** matrix. The algebraic symbols for parameter values and the error terms need not be entered. When the above problem is analyzed via multiple regression, the following estimates of parameters are obtained: $b_1 = 1.0$, $b_2 = 2.0$, $b_3 = 4.0$, and $b_4 = 5.0$. Again the multiple regression equation must be fit without a constant term, otherwise the set of predictor variables will not be independent. For these example data, the estimated proportion of variance accounted for (R^2) is equal to 1.00, as expected. Arc length estimates, obtained directly from the parameter values or by subtraction, are equal to those given in Figure 2.1, confirming the correctness of the procedure.

REFERENCES

ABDI, H., BARTHÉLEMY, J.-P., and LUONG, X. (1984) "Tree representations of associative structures in semantic and episodic memory research." In E. DeGreef and J. van Buggenhaut (Eds.), *Trends in Mathematical Psychology* (pp. 3-31). Amsterdam: North-Holland.

ALDENDERFER, M. S., and BLASHFIELD, R. K. (1984) *Cluster Analysis.* Sage University Paper series on Quantitative Applications in the Social Sciences, 07-44. Newbury Park, CA: Sage.

ARABIE, P., CARROLL, J. D., and DeSARBO, W. S. (1987) *Three-Way Scaling and Clustering.* Sage University Paper series on Quantitative Applications in the Social Sciences, 07-65. Newbury Park, CA: Sage.

ARABIE, P., and HUBERT, L. J. (1992) "Combinatorial data analysis." *Annual Review of Psychology, 43,* 169-203.

BARTHÉLEMY, J.-P., and GUÉNOCHE, A. (1991) *Tree Models of Proximity.* New York: John Wiley.

BUNEMAN, P. (1971) "The recovery of trees from measures of dissimilarity." In F. R. Hodson, D. G. Kendall, and P. Tautu (Eds.), *Mathematics in the Archaeological and Historical Sciences* (pp. 387-395). Edinburgh, UK: Edinburgh University Press.

CARROLL, J. D. (1976) "Spatial, non-spatial, and hybrid models for scaling." *Psychometrika, 41,* 439-463.

CARROLL, J. D. (1995) *Degenerate Solutions in the Nonmetric Fitting of a Wide Class of Models for Proximity Data.* Unpublished manuscript, Rutgers University.

CARROLL, J. D., and ARABIE, P. (1980) "Multidimensional scaling." In M. R. Rosenzweig and M. L. Porter (Eds.), *Annual Review of Psychology, 31,* 607-649.

CARROLL, J. D., and CHANG, J.-J. (1973) "A method for fitting a class of hierarchical tree structure models to dissimilarities data and its application to some body parts data of Miller's." *Proceedings, 81st Annual Convention, American Psychological Association, 8,* 1097-1098.

CARROLL, J. D., CLARK, L. A., and DeSARBO, W. S. (1984) "The representation of three-way proximities data by single and multiple tree structure models." *Journal of Classification, 1,* 25-74.

CARROLL, J. D., and CORTER, J. E. (1995) "A graph-theoretic method for organizing overlapping clusters into trees, multiple trees, or extended trees." *Journal of Classification, 12,* 283-313.

CARROLL, J. D., DeSARBO, W., and De SOETE, G. (1988) "Stochastic tree unfolding (STUN) models: Theory and applications." In H. H. Bock (Ed.), *Classification and Related Methods of Data Analysis* (pp. 421-430). Amsterdam: North-Holland.

CARROLL, J. D., DeSARBO, W., and De SOETE, G. (1989) "Two classes of stochastic tree unfolding models." In G. De Soete, H. Feger, and C. Klauer (Eds.), *New Developments in Psychological Choice Modeling* (pp. 161-176). Amsterdam: North-Holland.

CARROLL, J. D., and PRUZANSKY, S. (1975, July) "Fitting of hierarchical tree structure (HTS) models, mixtures of HTS models, and hybrid models, via mathematical programming and alternating least squares." Paper presented at the U.S.-Japan Seminar in Theory, Methods, and Applications of Multidimensional Scaling and Related Techniques, San Diego, CA.

CARROLL, J. D., and PRUZANSKY, S. (1980) "Discrete and hybrid scaling models." In E. D. Lantermann and H. Feger (Eds.), *Similarity and Choice* (pp. 108-139). Bern, Germany: Hans Huber.

COOMBS, C. H. (1964) *A Theory of Data.* New York: John Wiley.

CORTER, J. E. (1982) "ADDTREE/P: A PASCAL program for fitting additive trees based on Sattath and Tversky's ADDTREE algorithm." *Behavior Research Methods and Instrumentation, 14,* 353-354.

CORTER, J. E. (1989) "Extended tree representation of relationships among languages." In N. X. Luong (Ed.), *Analyse Arborée des Données Textuelles* [special issue]. *Cahiers des Utilisateurs de Machines Électronique ê des Fins d'Information et de Documentation (CUMFID), 16*(Juin), 139-155.

CORTER, J. E. (1992, June) "An order-N^3 algorithm for fitting additive trees." Paper presented at the annual meeting of the Classification Society of North America, East Lansing, MI.

CORTER, J. E. (1996) *A New Combinatoric Algorithm for Fitting Additive Trees.* Unpublished manuscript, Teachers College, Columbia University.

CORTER, J. E., and TVERSKY, A. (1986) "Extended similarity trees." *Psychometrika, 51,* 429-451.

CRITCHLEY, F., and HEISER, W. (1988) "Hierarchical trees can be perfectly scaled in one dimension." *Journal of Classification, 5,* 5-20.

CUNNINGHAM, J. P. (1978) "Free trees and bidirectional trees as representations of psychological distance." *Journal of Mathematical Psychology, 17,* 165-188.

DEGERMAN, R. L. (1970) "Multidimensional analysis of complex structure mixtures of class and quantitative variation." *Psychometrika, 35,* 475-491.

DeSARBO, W. S., MANRAI, A. K., and MANRAI, L. A. (1993) "Non-spatial tree models for the assessment of competitive market structure: An integrated review of the marketing and psychometric literatures." In J. Eliashberg and G. L. Lilien (Eds.), *Handbook in OR & MS, 5,* 193-257.

De SOETE, G. (1983) "A least squares algorithm for fitting additive trees to proximity data." *Psychometrika, 48,* 621-626.

De SOETE, G. (1984a) "Additive-tree representations of incomplete dissimilarity data." *Quality and Quantity, 18,* 387-393.

De SOETE, G. (1984b) "A least squares algorithm for fitting an ultrametric tree to a dissimilarity matrix." *Pattern Recognition Letters, 2,* 133-137.

De SOETE, G. (1984c) "Ultrametric tree representations of incomplete dissimilarity data." *Journal of Classification, 1,* 235-242.

De SOETE, G. (1986) "Optimal variable weighting for ultrametric and additive tree clustering." *Quality and Quantity, 20,* 169-180.

De SOETE, G. (1988) "Tree representations of proximity data by least squares methods." In H. H. Bock (Ed.), *Classification and Related Methods of Data Analysis* (pp. 147-156). Amsterdam: North-Holland.

De SOETE, G., and CARROLL, J. D. (1991) "Probabilistic multidimensional models of pairwise choice data." In F. G. Ashby (Ed.), *Multidimensional Models of Perception and Cognition* (pp. 61-88). Hillsdale, NJ: Lawrence Erlbaum.

De SOETE, G., and CARROLL, J. D. (in press) "Trees and other network models for representing proximity data." In P. Arabie, L. Hubert, and G. De Soete (Eds.), *Classification and Clustering*. River Edge, NJ: World Scientific.

De SOETE, G., CARROLL, J. D., and DeSARBO, G. W. (1987) "Least squares algorithms for constructing constrained ultrametric and additive tree representations of symmetric proximity data." *Journal of Classification, 4*, 155-174.

De SOETE, G., DeSARBO, G. W., and CARROLL, J. D. (1985) "Optimal variable weighting for hierarchical clustering: An alternating least-squares algorithm." *Journal of Classification, 2*, 173-192.

De SOETE, G., DeSARBO, G. W., FURNAS, G. W., and CARROLL, J. D. (1984) "The estimation of ultrametric and path length trees from rectangular proximity data." *Psychometrika, 49*, 289-310.

DOBSON, A. G. (1974) "Unrooted trees for numerical taxonomy." *Journal of Applied Probability, 11*, 32-42.

DYEN, I. (1962) "The lexicostatistically determined relationship of a language group." *International Journal of American Linguistics, 28*, 153-161.

EVERITT, B. (1980) *Cluster Analysis* (2nd ed.). New York: Wiley-Halsted.

FREEDMAN, D., and LANE, D. (1983) "Significance testing in a nonstochastic setting." In P. Bickel, K. Doksum, and J. L. Hodges, Jr. (Eds.), *Lehmann Festschrift* (pp. 185-208). Belmont, CA: Wadsworth.

FURNAS, G. W. (1980) *Objects and Their Features: The Metric Analysis of Two-Class Data*. Unpublished Ph.D. dissertation, Stanford University, Stanford, CA.

HAGE, P., and HARARY, F. (1983) *Structural Models in Anthropology*. Cambridge, UK: Cambridge University Press.

HARTIGAN, J. A. (1967) "Representation of similarity matrices by trees." *Journal of the American Statistical Association, 62*, 1140-1158.

HARTIGAN, J. A. (1975) *Clustering Algorithms*. New York: John Wiley.

HOLMAN, E. W. (1972) "The relation between hierarchical and Euclidean models for psychological distances." *Psychometrika, 37*, 417-423.

HOWE, E. S. (1988) "Dimensional structure of judgments of crimes." *Journal of Applied Social Psychology, 18*, 1371-1393.

HUTCHINSON, J. W. (1989) "NETSCAL: A network scaling algorithm for nonsymmetric proximity data." *Psychometrika, 54*, 25-51.

JACOBY, W. G. (1991) *Data Theory and Dimensional Analysis*. Sage University Paper series on Quantitative Applications in the Social Sciences, 07-78. Newbury Park, CA: Sage.

JAIN, A. K., and DUBES, R. C. (1988) *Algorithms for Clustering Data*. Englewood Cliffs, NJ: Prentice Hall.

JOHNSON, E. J., and TVERSKY, A. (1984) "Representations of perceptions of risks." *Journal of Experimental Psychology: General, 113*, 55-70.

JOHNSON, S. (1967) "Hierarchical clustering schemes." *Psychometrika, 32*, 241-254.

KLAUER, K. C. (1989) "Ordinal network representation: Representing proximities by graphs." *Psychometrika, 54*, 737-750.

KLAUER, K. C., and CARROLL, J. D. (1989) "A mathematical programming approach to fitting general graphs." *Journal of Classification, 6*, 247-270.

KRAUS, V. (1976) *Social Gradings of Occupations*. Unpublished Ph.D. dissertation, Hebrew University.

KRUSKAL, J. B. (1956) "On the shortest spanning subtree of a graph and the travelling salesman problem." *Proceedings of the American Mathematical Society, 7,* 48-50.

KRUSKAL, J. B., and WISH, M. (1978) *Multidimensional Scaling.* Sage University Paper series on Quantitative Applications in the Social Sciences, 07-11. Beverly Hills, CA: Sage.

LIEBETRAU, A. M. (1983) *Measures of Association.* Sage University Paper series on Quantitative Applications in the Social Sciences, 07-32. Beverly Hills, CA: Sage.

MILLER, G. A. (1969) "A psychological method to investigate verbal concepts." *Journal of Mathematical Psychology, 6,* 169-191.

MILLIGAN, G. (1989) "A validation study of a variable weighting algorithm for cluster analysis." *Journal of Classification, 6,* 53-71.

POWELL, M. J. D. (1977) "Restart procedures for the conjugate gradient method." *Mathematical Programming, 12,* 241-254.

PRUZANSKY, S., TVERSKY, A., and CARROLL, J. D. (1982) "Spatial vs. tree representations of proximity data." *Psychometrika, 47,* 3-24.

PUNJ, G., and STEWART, D. W. (1983) "Cluster analysis in marketing research: Review and suggestions for application." *Journal of Marketing Research, 20,* 134-148.

RESTLE, F. (1959) "A metric and an ordering on sets." *Psychometrika, 24,* 207-220.

ROSENBERG, S., and KIM, M. P. (1975) "The method of sorting as a data-gathering procedure in multivariate research." *Multivariate Behavioral Research, 10,* 489-502.

ROSKAM, E. E. (1973) *Fitting Ordinal Relational Data to a Hypothesized Structure* (Technical Report 73 MA 06). Nijmegen, The Netherlands: Catholic University, Department of Psychology.

SATTATH, S., and TVERSKY, A. (1977) "Additive similarity trees." *Psychometrika, 42,* 319-345.

SCHVANEVELD, R. W. (Ed.). (1990) *PATHFINDER Associative Networks: Studies in Knowledge Organization.* Norwood, NJ: Ablex.

SCOTT, J. (1991) *Social Network Analysis.* Newbury Park, CA: Sage.

SHEPARD, R. N. (1980) "Multidimensional scaling, tree-fitting, and clustering." *Science, 210,* 390-398.

SMITH, E. E., RIPS, L. J., SCHOBEN, E. J., ROSCH, E., & MERVIS, C. B. (1975). Unpublished data.

SNEATH, P., and SOKAL, R. (1973) *Numerical Taxonomy.* San Francisco: Freeman.

SWADESH, M. (1950) "Salish internal relationships." *International Journal of American Linguistics, 16,* 157-167.

TORGERSON, W. S. (1958) *Theory and Methods of Scaling.* New York: John Wiley.

TVERSKY, A. (1977) "Features of similarity." *Psychological Review, 84,* 327-352.

TVERSKY, A., and HUTCHINSON, W. (1986) "Nearest-neighbor analysis of psychological spaces." *Psychological Review, 93,* 3-22.

TVERSKY, A., and SATTATH, S. (1979) "Preference trees." *Psychological Review, 86,* 542-573.

WARD, J. H. (1963) "Hierarchical grouping to optimize an objective function." *Journal of the American Statistical Association, 58,* 236-244.

WINSBERG, S., and CARROLL, J. D. (1989) "A quasi-nonmetric method for multidimensional scaling via an extended Euclidean model." *Psychometrika, 54,* 217-230.

YOUNG, F. W. (1970) "Nonmetric multidimensional scaling: Recovery of metric information." *Psychometrika, 35,* 455-471.

YOUNG, F. W. (1980) "Quantitative analysis of qualitative data." *Psychometrika, 46,* 357-388.

ABOUT THE AUTHOR

JAMES E. CORTER is Associate Professor of Statistics and Education in the Department of Measurement, Evaluation, and Applied Statistics, Division of Psychology, Teachers College, Columbia University. Following undergraduate and graduate work at the University of North Carolina, Chapel Hill, he obtained his Ph.D. in Cognitive Psychology from Stanford University in 1983. His research interests include clustering and scaling methods, the psychology of judgment, similarity and categorization, teaching and learning of mathematical problem solving, and consumer behavior.